DC-8 & The Flying Tiger Line

Charles Kennedy & Guy Van Herbruggen

designed by Simon De Rudder

Jeffrey

*Classic jets forever!
Your friend Charlie Kennedy*

NY NY 30 June 2015

ACKNOWLEDGEMENTS

The authors would like to jointly thank
Simon De Rudder for his hard work
John Dickson and the Flying Tiger Line community
Charlie Straeche & Frank de Koster for providing the vast majority of the DC-8 pictures
John Wegg and Geoffrey Thomas for supplying some additional amazing DC-8 pictures
Carlos Soccio, Alex Edrei and John Attwood from the Pan Am International Flight Academy

from Charles Kennedy
Dino Carrera / Aviation News
Craig West & Tony Dixon / Airliner World
Enrique Perrella & John Wegg / Airways
Daria Ciesla / Invisible Hands Music
Ed Richards / The Airline Boutique
Brian Wiklem, David Thompson-Rowlands, Sam Chui, British Airways, Sally Kennedy and Julian Nowill for the encouragement, Edward Alice Lucy and Rob Crossing, Don and Heather Kennedy, Captain Adrian J. Potter, Captain Paul Bradd, Senior First Officer Ian Rowell
The chapter on the history of the Flying Tiger Line could not have been completed, or even attempted, without Art Chin's book Anything, Anytime, Anywhere (Tassles & Wings, 1993). I would also like to acknowledge Tiger Tales by Captain LeVerne J. Moldrem (Flying M Press, 1996). The chapter on the history of the DC-8 owes a great debt to Terry Waddington's book on the Douglas DC-8 (Great Airliners Volume 2, 1996) and George Walker Cearley Jr's self-published DC-8 pictoral history which today deservedly sells for over $100. Luckily I picked up a signed copy when it first came out in 1994 at The Airplane Shop in Miami for the price on the back cover. Thanks to these works I was able to write my own.

from Guy Van Herbruggen
Special thanks to Henri Fabry, Guy Viselé, Pierre Gillard, Jacque Barbé, Michael Prophet, John Emlet, Frans Van Humbeek, Stephen Cannaby and kudos to my wife France and my kids, Maria and José without whose encouragement and patience this book would not have been possible.

Charles Kennedy, Peter Kirschen, Eric Verlie and Guy Van Herbruggen
would like to jointly thank all the gofundme donors (anonymous or not) who have brought us within tantalising reach of our goal in particular Roger Van Poyer, King Hui, Xavier Jensen, Michel Vanderhaeghen, Olov Andersson, Torbjorn Okland, Andre Van Loon, Charles Van Herbruggen, Jean-Pierre Herinckx and the OFC Old Flyers Club of Belgium.

DC-8 And The Flying Tiger Line
Charles Kennedy and Guy Van Herbruggen
ISBN 978-0-9932604-0-7
© 2015 Astral Horizon Aviation Press. All rights reserved.
79 Wardour Street London W1D 6QB United Kingdom
www.theairlineboutique.com

CONTENTS

1. THE FLYING TIGER LINE — 7
2. THE DOUGLAS DC-8 — 23
3. HAPPY TIGER RECORDS — 42
4. INDIVIDUAL AIRCRAFT LIST — 43
5. FLIGHTDECK — 139
6. THE FLYING TIGERS DC-8-63 SIMULATOR — 155
7. THREE YEARS OFF THIS EARTH — 163
8. THE NASA DC-8 — 168

REFERENCES

Pictures (unless indicated)
All DC-8 aircraft pictures from Charlie Straeche & Frank de Koster collections / www.douglasdc8.com
All pictures on chapter 2 are from Douglas Aircraft Company
All cockpit pictures on chapter 5 from Guy Van Herbruggen
All pictures on chapter 7 from Mark Devereaux's photo book / www.flyingtigerline.org
Front cover picture by Douglas Aircraft Company via John Wegg
Back cover picture taken in Anchorage, courtesy by John Wegg

Other Books, periodicals and other publications
Flying Tiger Line DC-8 Operating Manual
Air Transport International (ATI) Cockpit Operations Manual
Douglas DC-8 - Lundkvist Aviation Research, 1983
Tigertrack - March 1999

Websites
www.dc-8jet.com - Fred Cox FTL DC-8 Fleet Information
www.justflight.com - DC-8 Jetliner Pilot's notes
www.airlinerlist.com/ - Servaas C. Verbrugge's DC-8 production list
www.flyingtigerline.org/ - various pages
www.ntsb.gov/investigations/AccidentReports/Pages/AAR7210.aspx - N785FT aviation accident report AAR-72-10
www.ntsb.gov/investigations/AccidentReports/Pages/AAR8408.aspx - N797FT aviation accident report AAR-84-08
www.ntsb.gov/Investigations/AccidentReports/Pages/AAR0707.aspx - N748UP aviation accident report AAR-07-07
www.ntsb.gov/investigations/AccidentReports/Pages/AAR9506.aspx - N782AL aviation accident report AAR-95-06
www.atsb.gov.au/publications/investigation_reports/1971/AAIR/aair197101202.aspx - CF-CPQ aviation accident report

1
THE FLYING TIGER LINE

Many cargo airlines over the years have done innovative work opening up the global supply chain and deserve their place in history - Lebanon's Trans Mediterranean, Seaboard World of the USA spring to mind, and of course today's monoliths Federal Express and UPS in the USA, not to mention the enormous cargo divisions of passenger carriers such as Cathay Pacific and Korean Air who operate enormous ranks of 747Fs. But none share the glamour, the pedigree, the history, the exotic origins, the poetry of the name: the Flying Tiger Line.

The story begins with Lieutenant General Claire Lee Chennault (September 6, 1893 - July 27, 1958) who learned to fly in World War 1 and remained in the service after the end of hostilities. He became head of the Pursuit Section of the Air Corps Tactical School and led the Army Air Corps aerobatic team The Three Musketeers (later known as Three Men On The Flying Trapeze) in the 1920s.

In April 1937 he left the Army Air Corps due to clashes with higher-ups and ill health (deafness and bronchial problems), and set sail for China, arriving two months later to train pilots flying for the Kuomintang, also known as the Chinese Nationalist Party, led by Chiang Kai-Shek, against Japan in the Second Sino-Japanese War.

Two return visits by Chennault from China to Washington to procure planes, supplies, and pilots for the war effort resulted in an unpublished presidential order from Franklin Roosevelt which provided one-hundred Curtiss P-40-B and -C Warhawks being sent across the Pacific to be based in Burma. The 300 American pilots and ground crew drawn from the US Navy (USN), Marine Corps (USMC) and US Air Force, then known as the United States Army Air Corps (USAAC) who went with them may not all have been idealists there to save China, but were mercenaries who wanted to fly and fight, and were definitely adventurers.

Under Chennault's command, and based in the Burmese capital of Rangoon and at Kunming inside China itself, they developed into a crack fighting force against the Japanese, and became a symbol of US military might in Asia. Although their formal name was the 1st American Volunteer Group or AVG, they became known as the Flying Tigers.

In the days after the Japanese attack on Pearl Harbour on December 7, 1941, pilots of the AVG intercepted ten Japanese fighter aircraft inbound to attack Kunming and shot down four of them, thereby striking the USA's first blow against Japan post-Pearl Harbour.

The success of the AVG led them to being brought into the USAAF. Chennault was reinstated as a colonel and immediately promoted to Brigadier General commanding USAAF units initially designated the China Air Task Force and later the Fourteenth Air Force.

Due to some disagreements about the way AVG pilots were to be incorporated into the USAAF, most AVG pilots left the unit and went on to fly freight over the eastern Himalayas from India to China (known as The Hump) to continue the struggle on behalf of Chinese nationalists, or joined the 23rd Fighter Group.

Despite the Allied position deteriorating in China and losses through attrition, the Flying Tigers' record in battle was extraordinary - despite lacking resources, the AVG's kill ratio was the highest of any contemporary Allied air group in the Pacific theatre, with 115 Japanese aircraft shot down or destroyed on the ground, with the loss of around 300 enemy lives; fourteen AVG pilots were killed in action, including six killed in accidents and two in enemy bombing raids. Improvisation was key and Chennault was able to shift unsuitable pilots to staff jobs and vice versa, as the AVG had no ranks, so there was no division between officers and enlisted personnel. Their success against the odds was attributed to high morale and esprit de corps in a team of highly capable volunteer pilots, which would remain a hallmark of every flying operation to bear the Flying Tiger name.

Robert William Prescott (May 5, 1914 - March 3, 1978) was born in Fort Worth, Texas, and moved as a teenager to California where he studied at Compton Junior College and drove trucks to pay the bills. He went on to study at the Loyola Law School in the Los Angeles suburb of Westlake when he got the flying bug visiting the naval flying school at Long Beach Airport. In 1939, two years ahead of the US entry into World War 2, he quit law school and enlisted in the United States Navy as a pilot. By 1941 he was an instructor at the naval flying school in Pensacola, Florida, when he volunteered to fight the communists in China and joined the clandestine AVG.

After the incorporation of the AVG back into the USAAF, he flew briefly for TWA as co-pilot including the "Mission To Moscow" flight, carrying US ambassador Joseph E Davies to deliver a secret letter from President Roosevelt to Soviet leader Joseph Stalin. He soon left TWA and joined the China National Airways Corporation flying trips over The Hump to continue the war effort alongside the India-China Division of the Air Transport Command (ATC).

Back in California at the end of the war, Prescott met a group of businessmen headed by oil magnate and commercial fruit grower Samuel B. Mosher who were interested in founding an all-cargo airline, mainly to fly perishable goods from Mexico to the western USA. A deal was struck whereby Mosher would match whatever funds Prescott was able to raise. The new company was called National Skyway Freight Corporation, and formally incorporated in the state of Delaware on June 25, 1945.

In short order, Prescott recruited nine Flying Tigers from the AVG: Richard Rossi, Ernest "Bus" Loane, Robert J. "Catfish" Raine, Joseph Rosbert, William Bartling, Clifford Groh, C. H. "Link" Laughlin, Thomas Haywood, and Robert Hedman. With contributions from the pilots (including $10,000 from Rossi) and two ground crew, Prescott raised $89,000 which was duly matched by Mosher.

National Skyway's first office was in the Biltmore Hotel on Pershing Square in downtown Los Angeles, but soon relocated to the terminal building at Long Beach airport.

Prescott's search for suitable hardware to begin flight operations turned up an unusual candidate: the RB-1 Conestoga, built by the Budd Company of Philadelphia, better known as a supplier of parts to the auto industry and for manufacturing stainless steel rail carriages.

The Conestoga, which first flew on October 31, 1943, was able to get airborne with a payload of 10,400 lbs (4,700 kg) after a takeoff roll of just 920 feet (280 metres) but the huge wing resulted in high fuel burn and a range of just 650 miles (1,050 km) which reduced it's appeal, especially given the advent of the world-beating C-47 from Douglas. The USAAF cancelled it's order for 600 Conestogas completely, and the Navy reduced it's order from 200 to just twenty-five, so the Conestoga did not find a role in World War 2.

However, the seventeen surviving machines were sold by the War Assets Administration (WWA) for $28,642 each (the going rate at the time for a C-47 was around $100,000) to the fledgling National Skyway.

Initial contracts were to fly fresh produce from California to the east coast, with empty capacity on the return flight used to transport furniture made in New York for sale in California.

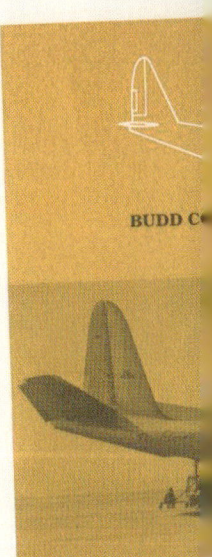

Early pioneering...
The Budd Conestoga, Flyin[g] stainless steel, rear-loading, [com]pany that had made its reput[ation] questioned its looks and ever[...] fly. But it did, starting with [...] 1945, when Robert W. Pres[cott] nally built for the U.S. Nav[y...] of cargo at about 150 mile[s...] airline's headquarters in th[e...] Long Beach Municipal Air[port...] field produce shipper, was [...] plane-loads of fresh grape[s...] airline off the ground — lite[rally...]

BUDD C[O]

The airline's first revenue flights all took place on August 21, 1945, on behalf of the California Fruit Growers' Association, flying flowers to Detroit, grapes to Atlanta, and furniture from New York.

The second westbound flight full of furniture was forced to make a belly landing in a graveyard shortly after takeoff in Detroit due to a technical fault with the aircraft; although none of the crew were hurt, the first officer walked away from scene and from flying altogether - so the story goes, he was never heard from again. The Conestoga was, in the words of Prescott, "mechanically precarious", and two more were lost before the type's retirement, one in Virginia and one in Albuquerque (admittedly the last accident caused by crew fatigue rather than a fault with the aircraft).

DOUGLAS C-54 1947-1957

In October of the same year, National Skyway was chosen to fly 117 sailors home to New York, which was completed using five Conestogas piloted by Prescott, Tom Haywood, Cliff Groh, Joe Rosbert, and Duke Hedman, all ex-AVG flyers. This was the airline's first-ever passenger service.

The Conestogas were becoming a technical nightmare - in a likeable euphemism, one became "mechanically inoperative" in a Texan field - but luckily war surplus Douglas C-47s and Curtiss C-46s were becoming available at affordable rates, and by June 1946 the last seven Conestogas were gone, replaced by sixteen C-47s and soon after that, C-54s, the military version of the four-engined DC-4.

In early 1946 National Skyway relocated to Mine Field (later LAX). By now the airline had manned stations at San Francisco, Cleveland, New York, Chicago, Detroit and St Louis.

1947 started with a breakthrough, when the US military Air Transport Command awarded National Skyway a transpacific airlift contract on New Year's Day. The contract had previously been fulfilled by United Airlines, but with the post-war economy booming, United decided to focus on scheduled domestic passenger operations. The contract entailed twenty-eight weekly flights in support of US forces in Hawaii, across the Pacific, and Japan, and paid 28¢ a mile, all originating from Fairfield Army Base (today Travis AFB) to Honolulu, Kwajalein, Guam and Tokyo.

The very next day was moving day; after just nine months at Mine Field, the airline's base was relocated to a hangar with adjoining office space at the Lockheed Air Terminal at Burbank airport in the northern suburbs of Los Angeles on January 2.

Thirty-two C-54 aircraft were supplied to National Skyway by the Air Transport Command to fulfil the Pacific contract, and this most momentous month in the airline's history ended with the change of name from National Skyway Freight Corporation to the words that already decorated the rear fuselage of every

1945-1947

aircraft in the fleet from the Conestogas onwards: the Flying Tiger Line.

Other cargo operators were springing up, encouraged by a strong economy and the abundant availability of war-surplus aircraft - Flamingo Air Service, Mutual Aviation, California Eastern Airways, Willis Air Service, Air Cargo Transport, Globe Freight Airline, US Airlines, Air News, and the better-known Slick Airways.

All these and more applied to the CAB (Civil Aeronautics Board, which performed some of the duties of today's FAA) for scheduled route licences in what was in those days an extremely highly-regulated marketplace compared to the deregulated markets of today. Tiger was given temporary authorisation to fly from Burbank and San Francisco to Seattle, Portland, Cleveland, Chicago, Detroit, St Louis, Dayton, Dallas, Oklahoma City, New York, Philadelphia and Allentown. In reality, however, at this point Tiger only flew to eight cities: Burbank, New York, San Francisco, Detroit, Cleveland, Chicago, Kansas City and St Louis, and employed fifty people in flight ops, thirty-one in ground ops, 114 in maintenance, thirty-one in sales and traffic, and twenty-two in executive roles.

At the end of 1947, Prescott had the following to say about the future of his industry in a letter to James Landis, chairman of the CAB, thus: "Perhaps some of us are overly optimistic. Certainly I will say to you that optimism and an almost blind faith in the future have been two requisites to us who have persisted in this business. But I visualise great fleets of cargo planes moving about our country in the not-too-distant future. Surely it is true that in every other form of transportation, the volume of freight movement has far exceeded that of passengers."

At the end of the CAB's deliberations, on July 29, 1949, Flying Tiger Line was awarded the first all-cargo freight licence, Route 100, from California to New York via points across the US. By the beginning of 1950 Tiger was serving seventeen cities between Burbank and Boston. In the same year, the C-47s were replaced by C-46 Commandos, which were bigger, heavier, with greater performance and available payload. With the War Assets Administration sitting on 625 of them, some with as few as ten hours on the airframe, they also had the advantage of being cheap to acquire.

On June 25, 1950, the Korean War broke out when North Korean president Kim Il-Sung attempted to reunify the Korean peninsula by force after it's division by the USA and USSR in 1945 following the defeat of Japan at the end of World War 2 into two countries, North and South Korea. Within twenty-four hours of the Military Air Transport Service (MATS) requisitioning commercial aircraft, Tiger had the first civilian aircraft in the war effort en route to Japan and by August accounted for ten percent of the civilian airlift flying for MATS. The airlift to Tokyo, using C-54s, followed two primary routes: from McChord AFB near Tacoma, Washington across the arc of the Aleutian Islands to Japan, and from Fairfield AFB near San Francisco across the central Pacific via Hawaii, the Marshall Islands and Micronesia. A third of the payload was passenger, and two-thirds freight.

Don Downie told Wings in April 1990, "Long overwater flights at night during that period were still regarded with a certain degree of trepidation, particularly over the vast expanse of the Pacific, where landmarks were non-existent and friendly airports few. It took a reliable aircraft like the C-54 to make intercontinental overwater flight in variable weather, at night, a near non-event. The C-54 had a maximum 20,000 lb (9,071 kg) payload, and the fast turnaround and short on-the-ground time made the C-54 so efficient on those Pacific airlifts."

Between 1951 and 1953, Tiger received 48.1%, 42.5% and 48% of it's revenue from the Pacific airlift respectively. The income in dollar terms for 1952 from the Pacific was over $12.3m. In the same period, the payroll increased from 528 employees in January 1951 to 1,650 by June 1952. The main MATS route was between Fairfield AFB to Tokyo, operating about fifty times each month. Other busy routes in the Korean War period included flying twice daily from New York to Oakland on behalf of the US Navy, and transporting payloads of aero engines and other aviation-related payloads from San Antonio to bases in the Midwest and Pacific. Tiger also landed a lucrative $2½m contract to overhaul 100 military-operated C-46 Commandos.

As the airline expanded, it built a new two-storey corporate HQ a couple of blocks from the perimeter of Burbank Airport where their offices had been next door to the Tiger hangar, and the move took place in early 1951.

Meanwhile, Claire Chennault's post-war commercial airline operation in Taiwan, Civil Air Transport, opened an office called Aviation Parts And Equipment Inc at Burbank to sell fifty war surplus C-46s plus a handful of C-47s, which were all refurbished in the Tiger hangar. Thirteen of the C-46s were bought by Tiger and sold on to Riddle Airlines for a profit of $350,000. At the end of a busy year, Tiger placed the biggest order for new planes by any cargo airline ever, for seven DC-6As from Douglas, at a total cost of $7 million. This was Tiger's first acquisition of non-military surplus aircraft, and as such represented symbolically a big step forward.

Outside of the military sphere, Tiger found other ways to deploy it's fleet, such as transporting American students to Europe for study and holidays, European migrants to Australia, farm labourers from Puerto Rico to the US, undocumented Mexicans from the US back to Mexico, USAF cadets to training details and trainee mechanics and engineers to Tiger's own base at Burbank where third party training was on offer.

After the war in Korea had been fought to a stalemate with an armistice signed at Panmunjom inside the DMZ (Demilitarised Zone) on the border between the two Koreas on July 27, 1953, Tiger showed it's usual resourcefulness at finding other work for it's fleet, such as ferrying aircraft parts and engines from Wright Patterson AFB at Dayton to England, France, and Morocco. With two-hundred sales agents around the world, by April 1955, twenty Tiger planes were deployed on contract work throughout Asia, Europe, and the Caribbean, and eight more planes were flying domestic trooping flights for the Army in a programme known as the Civilian Army Movement System (CAMS). Scheduled domestic operations included a dozen flights a day between San Francisco, Burbank, Seattle and New York, with up to twenty-five intermediate station stops.

The middle of the 1950s were turbulent times, with a failed merger attempt with Slick Airways, and a 114-day strike by Tiger machinists and other personnel in 1955. Some stability returned with the delivery of the first DC-6As, enabling the opening of a daily San Francisco to Chicago nonstop, a Burbank-Chicago-Detroit-New York service. The CAB renewed Tiger's Route 100 authority for another five years on March 12, 1956, and the Post Office gave Tiger the authority to carry airmail, which took place for the first time on May 28.

Tiger played a significant role in one of the world's unsung technical accomplishments, the construction of fifty radar installations along a barren 3,000 mile (4,828km) frontier from Alaska to Baffin Island, which became known as the Dew Line, D-E-W standing for Distant Early Warning, designed to detect the approach of enemy aircraft from over the pole, part of the extensive North American Air Defence Command (NORAD) system.

The supply mission required the services of fifty Canadian and thirty-one American commercial airlines working in lightly-mapped polar areas under extreme Arctic conditions including compass deviations, visual 'white-out', and upside-down mirages floating above the horizon. Tiger made the largest contribution of any US airline, with seven planes operating out of Churchill in the eastern sector and eleven planes operating out of Hay River in the western sector. Although seven Tiger planes were lost in the two-year project, no personnel were killed or injured.

A major order was placed for twelve of Lockheed's triple-tailed L-1049-H (the cargo version of the -G) Super Constellations later the same year, worth $20million to Lockheed, who were just metres away on the same airfield at Burbank. The Connies were all delivered in 1957.

A North Atlantic passenger charter business had built up in the mid-50s using the DC-6As. Tiger was the biggest independent air carrier across the pond by 1956, with bases at Gander and Frankfurt and a passenger ticket office in Geneva, and with the advent of the Super Connies the business escalated - in 1957 Tiger carried 70,000 passengers across the ocean. As leisure traffic was seasonal, other opportunities to earn revenue were found, such as a political crisis in Lebanon one September requiring the eastbound movement of US forces and materiel, while most Tiger passenger traffic at that time of year was returning westbound to the US.

Although pure jets were considered as early as the mid-50s, Tiger stuck with props for a little longer, by ordering thirteen Canadair CL-44D-4-2s, at a cost of $3.8 million each (versus $7 million for a new Boeing 707). The CL-44D was a Bristol Britannia built under licence in Canada, with some modifications including a stretch of 12 feet 4 inches (3.75 metres). Although the type was not a major success with only thirty-nine built (and indeed Bristol only built eighty-five Britannias), US cargo airlines gave it a niche, with eight ordered by Seaboard World and four by Slick Airways. Twelve were built as CC-106 Yukons for the Royal Canadian Air Force. The only other customer was Icelandic passenger carrier Loftleidir who flew six with a type name of Rolls-Royce 400, which led to the CL-44 sometimes being known as the Canadair 400.

The CL-44D was the first large aircraft with a true 'swing-tail', which could be opened in just ninety seconds, making loading and loading much easier than via side cargo doors (which the CL-44D also had). The type's operating cost advantage over the Super Connie was calculated to be as high as 40%. The first one was delivered to Burbank on June 2, 1961. This was the first time the famous circled T logo appeared on the tail of a Tiger aircraft.

March 1962 saw the opening of a $1½ million freight terminal at Chicago O'Hare airport with fourteen loading docks. With the palletised loading system on the CL-44Ds, a full aircraft's payload of 62,000 lbs could be unloaded and loaded in one hour and fifteen minutes, compared to 46,000 lbs with a Super Connie which used a bulk loading method that took at least three, and sometimes up to to five hours to complete.

However that wasn't enough of an operational efficiency saving, and Tiger began looking to join the jet age. An ambitious order was placed for eight Lockheed L-300 Super Starlifters, the civil version of the C-141 Starlifter, which would have incorporated straight-in, truck-bed level rear loading and an all-up payload of 70,000 lbs. However, Lockheed stated that they would only commit to building the L-300 with total orders for fifty machines, which was never attained, and Tiger's $500,000 deposit was returned.

In 1962 the Sea-Air programme, also known as Sea Tiger, was launched, an intermodal transport service which involved freight crossing the Pacific by sea from Japan to the Port of Los Angeles, being trucked or flown across the US mainland, then flown to Europe or South America. This sped up high-value shipments and more importantly gave customers a single bill of lading for their goods all the way from Asia to a far off destination on the other side of the world.

The Flying Tiger line joined the jet age with the delivery of their first Boeing 707-349C, N322F on September 27, 1965; it's sister ship, N323F, arrived on October 13. Robert Prescott celebrated his airline's latest tool of the trade by sending lobsters to the CAB, with a note: "Now you can ship lobsters cheaper than mail"!

Tiger wasted no time in flexing it's muscles with it's latest hardware, by flying N322F around the world between November 14 and 17, 1965, setting records, setting records en route including fastest pole-to-pole speed. The flight positioned from Palm Springs in the desert east of Los Angeles to Honolulu, then, with the stopwatch ticking, flew over the North Pole to London, on to Lisbon en route to Buenos Aires, over the South Pole to Christchurch in New Zealand and finally back to Honolulu. The aircraft was then positioned back to Burbank. The Honolulu to Honolulu trip spent fifty-seven hours and twenty-seven minutes in the air and a total elapsed block time of sixty-two hours, twenty-seven minutes and thirty-five seconds.

The flight was commanded by Captain Fred L. Austin, with Captains Harrison Finch and Robert N. Buck, all of TWA, along with Flying Tigers chief pilot Jack Martin. The flight carried three flight engineers - Dino Valezza and James M. Jones of TWA, and Tiger's own Eugene Olson. Such an ambitious flight also carried three navigators - two freelancers, John Larsen and Lauran DeGroot, and Tiger's E. A. Hickman. (Polar navigation is a very demanding science - every direction from the North Pole is south and vice versa, so finding the pole is easy but getting out of it in a direction that will take you somewhere you want to go is a complex business.)

The flight also carried twenty-three passengers and press, a mixed group including members of The Explorers Club, the US Weather Bureau, the vice-president of the Union Bank of Los Angeles, researchers from the Douglas Aircraft Company's space division, NYU, NASA, photographers from Life magazine, Los Angeles TV personality Clete Roberts, and Father Anderson Bakewell of Washington DC's Holy Trinity Church.

For Prescott, the triumph was overshadowed by tragedy; while the aircraft was on the ground in London, he learned that his twelve year-old son Peter Prescott had been killed in a Lear Jet crash in Palm Springs. (Five years later, Bob Prescott opened the Peter Prescott Childrens Hospital in honour of his son, in Taiwan.)

As the Vietnam War escalated, Tiger leased two further 707-349Cs from Boeing, which were delivered in June 1966 and February 1967 respectively, fulfilling new contracts on behalf of the Military Airlift Command (MAC, having been renamed from MATS on January 1, 1966). The main bases used by Tiger during the conflict were Norton AFB and Travis AFB in California, and McChord AFB in Washington State; in the Pacific they were Hickham AFB in Hawaii, and Guam; along the north Pacific, flights touched down in Cold Bay, Elmendorf AFB or Anchorage; in Japan, Kadena AFB at Okinawa, Tachikawa AFB and Yokota AFB; Udon and Khorat AFB in Thailand; Clark AFB in the Philippines; and Osan AFB in South Korea. Main bases in Vietnam itself were at Bien Hoa, Saigon (Tan San Nhut), Cam Ranh Bay, and Da Nang. Tiger had personnel at each station as well as local staff including Vietnamese inside South Vietnam.

The total commitment to the airlift involved a huge range of operations, such as flying massive amounts of materiel on cargo flights, trooping flights from the US to the theatre of combat, and R&R (rest and recuperation) trips out of the theatre to places such as Singapore, Hawaii, Bangkok, Taiwan, the Philippines, Australia, New Zealand and Japan.

The whole operation was co-ordinated through the Flight Planning Centre at Yokota AFB, thirty miles

A Military Aircraft Command MAC charter flight aboard a DC-8 in 1976

For Captain Ted Brondum, this was the uniform of the day during the Ricelift to Phnom Penh in the spring of 1975

outside Tokyo, which was a major maintenance base, and where crews were changed. The February 1971 edition of Flying Tiger Line's in-house publication Tigerview sets the scene:

"Yokota is a buzzing beehive of activity. From it's $85,000 structure housing operations, administrative and maintenance staff and functions, FTL handles not only its own flights but similarly supports under contract a number of other carriers flying for MAC. There are days when we handle a dozen or more aircraft and months when the 30-a-day figure goes as high as 350.

The FTL people at Yokota meet all incoming charter aircraft on a strict first-come-first-served basis. And a fleet of half-a-dozen radio-controlled station wagons and microbuses keeps busy shuttling Tiger and other airline crews back and forth, from aircraft to Japanese customs and immigration to hotels in the surrounding area.

In addition, Tiger crews are moved regularly between Yokota and Tokyo International Airport [Haneda] to comply with the daily flight schedules prepared and sent out by headquarters. Add to these the flight personnel from other airlines and the grand total can amount to as many as 250 crew members, often spread out from Yokota to Tokyo to Yokohama. The hotel woes were made even greater throughout 1970 by thousands of tourists flocking to Expo '70 in Osaka."

By 1969 the 707s were gone and the airline was operating a fleet of seventeen newly-acquired Douglas DC-8-63Fs. Even without the massive war effort in southeast Asia, US imports to the Pacific Rim grew at an average rate of 58% per year between 1962 and 1966, and continued at 40% per year in the period of 1966-1971, and 16% from 1971 to 1977, so Tiger's attention was very much on the Pacific as it expanded with new DC-8 deliveries.

In September 1969 Tiger was finally awarded the coveted Route 163 licence for scheduled transpacific flying, originating in Los Angeles with stops in San Francisco, Seattle and Anchorage on the way to Tokyo, Naha (Okinawa), Taipei, Hong Kong and Seoul, with service soon extended to Osaka, Manila, Hong Kong and Bangkok.

A new Tiger facility was constructed at Tokyo International Airport - a two-storey structure with a 4,250 square foot warehouse, and a 940 square foot mezzanine which served as a flight dispatch facility for all commercial (non-MAC) flights through Japan, taking some pressure off Yokota AFB.

Tiger expanded not only in the Pacific but at home as well. At the start of the decade, the airline flew scheduled service to Los Angeles, San Francisco, Portland, Seattle, Milwaukee, Chicago, Detroit, Cleveland, Buffalo, Syracuse, Binghamton, Hartford, Boston, New York (Kennedy and Newark), and Philadelphia.

As well as putting new points on the map, Tiger expanded and renewed it's ground infrastructure. As the 70s dawned, the freight terminals at both Los Angeles and San Francisco doubled in size; the San Francisco facility consisted of a World War 2-era Pan Am hangar divided into two, with one half used for maintenance and the other with enough room to accommodate a DC-8-63F loading while completely under cover. In Detroit, a brand new $2.25 million facility was constructed, and Boston and Newark were also substantially expanded in the same period.

In New York $1.2 million was spent on a processing centre for international cargo was built out on 150th Street to take some pressure off the existing facility, followed by a new 90,250 square foot warehouse and office building on a 10-acre site on the airfield, at a cost of $6.4 million, opening in September 1972.

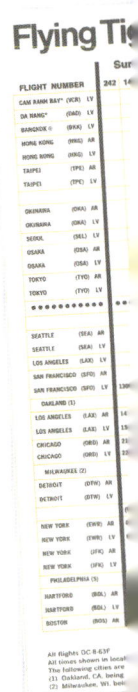

The following year, 1972, saw the completion of High Tiger, a ten-storey corporate headquarters at 7401 World Way West, with 104,000 square feet of office space overlooking Los Angeles International Airport.

While Tiger expanded, other airlines wound down their cargo business. Continental, Delta and Eastern all ended their dedicated freight operations in 1973, mostly as a result of the increased belly space in their new widebody passenger jets, DC-10s in the case of Continental and Lockheed L-1011s at Delta and Eastern.

Even as the Vietnam War was winding down, Tiger extended Route 163 with scheduled service to Saigon after Pan Am cancelled flights in a bilateral spat with the South Vietnamese authorities who wanted their small airline Air Vietnam to have transpacific route licences.

In the closing stages of the war, Cambodia was in distress as the Khmer Rouge, led by Pol Pot, had managed to cut all supply lines to the country. To feed the population of the capital, Phnom Penh, Tiger flew 176 flights from Saigon to Pochentong airport where landing aircraft ran the gauntlet of exploding rockets and artillery during twenty-minute turnarounds, bringing 16,687,265 lbs (7,569 tonnes) of rice. The flights ended on April 12, 1975 with the fall of Phnom Penh to the advancing Khmer Rouge.

Only days later, the last remnants of South Vietnam were captured by the People's Army of Vietnam, more widely known as the Viet Cong. In the final days of the war, Tiger operated rescue flights to move Vietnamese refugees out of harm's way, and in many cases to new lives, as a major player in Operation Frequent Wind, the evacuation of US forces, dependants, and local allies from Saigon.

While the outcome of the conflict in Korea was judged to be a victory as the border between the two Koreas stayed intact after the end of the war, whereas the fall of South Vietnam and the reunification of the country under communist rule was considered to be a defeat for the USA, with the passing of time perhaps an opposite view is more appropriate, as North Korea, trauma-

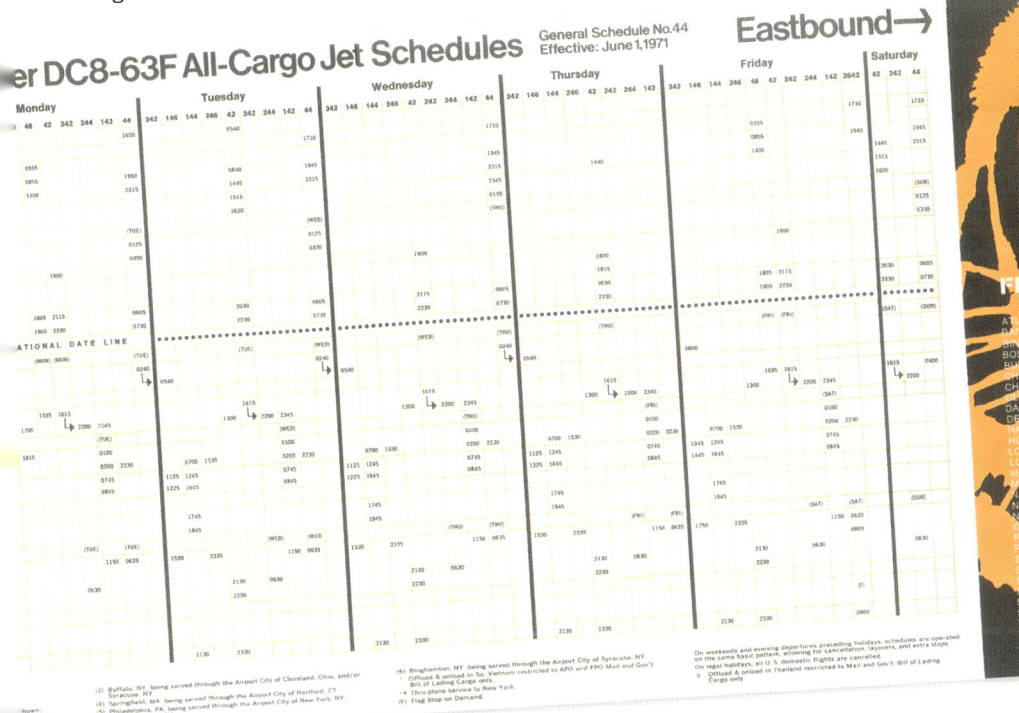

tised by the conflict and withdrawn from the world, is a volatile and mysterious hot potato even after more than sixty years, whereas Vietnam today is a peaceful and open nation with good relations with the outside world including it's former nemesis in the west.

Tiger joined the 'widebody club' with the arrival of N800FT, an ex-American Airlines 747-123, on August 28, 1974, followed by N801FT a month later from the same source. These were passenger liners that were converted to freighters at Boeing's facility at Wichita. Tiger ended up operating twenty-eight 747s in their own livery or with FT registration suffixes, with another six on a more temporary basis. Only four were ordered new with Flying Tiger Line customer codes, N806FT, N807FT, N808FT and N810FT, 747-249Fs delivered between October 31, 1979 and September 12, 1980. Two more 747s arrived from the production line in 1980,

ordered by Seaboard World but delivered new to Flying Tiger after the merger of the two airlines, which was completed on October 1, 1980.

As the first 747s came online, the DC-8s became domestic workhorses while the jumbos plied the long routes to Asia in competition with Japan Air Lines and Northwest Orient who were also prolific operators of 747Fs. The huge aeroplanes brought massive efficiency to Tiger; as early as 1969, Aviation Week & Space Technology magazine made an analysis of Tiger operations and calculated that the CL-44D cost 6.71¢ per available ton-mile, the 707-320C and DC-8-63F about 3.66¢, and the 747, then in the future, would cost about 2.75¢.

The 747-200Fs that were delivered new had the added advantage of a nose section that opened vertically, allowing unloading and loading during ground-stops of only ninety minutes, and with so much built-in automation that this task could be attained with only the same number of personnel as needed to turn a DC-8, despite handling twice the payload.

More infrastructure was added towards the end of the 1970s, with a $4 million cargo facility and ramp extension at Anchorage, through which almost all of Tiger's Asia flights routed, for fuelling, crew changes, and freight transloading between flights, making the Alaskan city a 'scissor hub' for Tiger.

Hong Kong became a major transloading hub when the Hong Kong Air Cargo Terminal (HACTL) opened in 1978, a $23 million project created by a consortium of local firms in collaboration with the regional government of the British colony. Tiger was given a dispensation to receive and document it's own cargo there, with HACTL providing packing, staging and loading. Hong Kong received five Tiger 747s and two DC-8s a week, some of which were timed to coincide with Cathay Pacific 707F flights onward to Singapore, providing US exporters with same day all-cargo service to a city which, despite being only 225 square miles of territory and 2.5 million people, was the second-biggest importer of US goods after Japan (although admittedly much of this was re-exported).

As part of the interline agreement, Cathay also provided onward 707F service to Seoul three days a week, and twice a week to Kuala Lumpur. Tiger also interlined at the HACTL with Malaysia Airlines (MAS) to Penang, Royal Brunei to Bandar Seri Begawan, Garuda Indonesia to Jakarta, and Swissair to Bangkok.

1978 started with a tragedy for the Flying Tiger family, as their founder, leader and inspiration, Robert Prescott, passed away at home in Palm Springs on March 3, aged only 64. He was the company's only president and chief executive in his lifetime. He participated in five major campaigns in China while serving with the AVG and becoming an ace with 5¼ kills, then turning tiny National Skyway, "the Flying Tiger line", into a global brand, honoured in his lifetime as a "Giant In Air Transportation" by the Smithsonian Institute. With such a record, there is no question that Prescott was one of America's greatest-ever aviators, and now he was gone.

From March 6 to March 10, the stars and stripes was flown at half-mast throughout the Tiger system. On March 11, the story of his accomplishments were incorporated into the Congressional Record in session in Washington DC. On August 14, the High Tiger headquarters tower at LAX was dedicated the memory of the company's beloved founder, as was the first factory-fresh 747-249F Freightmaster when it was delivered from Seattle to Los Angeles on November 2.

In October 1978, the deregulation of the US domestic airline market which Prescott had fought for to create new markets for his company finally took effect, and with the abolition of the CAB, Tiger expanded rapidly into markets it had coveted for years, most notably local service from the 'Lower 48' to Alaska (previously all traffic to Alaska was only stopping for fuel or transloading between aeroplanes). Other sought-after markets to come online were Miami, Charlotte, Atlanta, San Juan, the US Virgin Islands, Dallas and Houston. By 1979, according to IATA numbers, the Flying Tiger Line was the world's number one cargo carrier outside of the Soviet Union's monolithic Aeroflot, overtaking Pan Am.

Around the same time Tiger expanded it's door-to-door service, although did not emphasise the express document and small package service which was the domain of Federal Express and UPS, but

offered the services of a traditional freight forwarder, with pick-up and drop-off by independent trucking services bolted on to the core Tiger product. The slogan for the product was "It's on time. Or it's on us."

The airline continued to excel at meeting it's "Anything, Anytime, Anywhere" promise by transporting one-hundred and twenty-two wild animals from San Francisco to the Koizumi African Safari Park in Fukuoka, Japan (including thirty-seven tigers, thirty-three lions, nine bears); engines for installation on other airlines' stranded jumbo jets; telephone poles; racehorses; railway cars; Shamu the killer whale; a helicopter for use in a James Bond movie, on the tailboom of which was placed a small Tiger logo in gratitude for it's safe transport to the filming location; 100,000 lbs of fresh produce every week all the way from Seattle to the Persian Gulf statelet of Qatar where the Doha Supermarket, thanks to the Flying Tiger, could offer the same range of consumer luxury as any outlet in the USA. A real tiger called Gombi was flown to the Philippines to appear in the Vietnam-set movie Apocalypse Now, and camera equipment, explosives and a helicopter went along too.

The 1980 merger with Seaboard World brought Europe into the fold, where Tiger had flown since the 1950s but not in the way it had prioritised Asia. Seaboard's flights beyond Europe to Bahrein in the Persian Gulf and their sales office in Lebanon were seen by Tiger as a possible stepping-stone to a round-the-world service. The merger itself was accomplished painlessly as a formula was found for Seaboard employees to retain their seniority, and the two airlines were quickly one.

The Seaboard merger brought with it passenger route licences, and a bookable scheduled airline operation was begun in 1981 alongside the more traditional MAC trooping flights. To preserve the Flying Tiger Line brand as cargo-only, the new project was named Metro International Airlines and scheduled flights were operated to Brussels, plus charters to Athens, Lisbon, Tel Aviv, and various points in Europe and the Caribbean, using a trio of second-hand Boeing 747-212Bs that had been bought from Singapore Airlines. Three classes of service were offered: business class called Captain's Deck on the upper deck; a product that today would be recognised as premium economy called Metropolitan Class in the nose and forward cabin, and Economy class for the rest of the main deck.

One of the less favourable consequences of the Seaboard World merger was the shouldering of a large debt burden, which made the hoped-for synergies hard to come by. In addition, a host of domestic competitors began appearing. By 1983 Tiger was up against Airborne Air Freight with twenty-one aircraft based in Wilmington Ohio; Burlington Express with thirteen aircraft based in Fort Wayne Indiana; CF Airfreight with sixteen aircraft based at Indianapolis; Emery Air Freight with forty-two aircraft based at Dayton; and UPS with eighty-five aircraft based at Louisville. Many of these were enabled by very low purchase and conversion costs for first generation jetliners as passenger carriers upgraded their original 707 and DC-8 fleets with new widebodies such as the DC-10 and L-1011 or Boeing's latest 757 and 767 products. Some of the competition's DC-8s were even acquired directly from Tiger as the airline sold some of it's fleet in an effort to find a 'right size'.

In 1983 the decision was made to get out of the passenger-carrying business. The three Metro International 747-212Bs were swapped to Pan Am in return for four 747-121Fs plus four spare engines and a store of spare parts, a deal that suited both parties as Pan Am was every bit as keen to get out of the business of running dedicated freighters as Tiger was to focus exclusively on it.

One of Metro's biggest clients, Tower Travel, went into the airline business to fill the gap to create JFK-based Tower Air which started flying the same year Metro was closed down, and spent the next seventeen years flying it's all 747 Classic (-100 and -200) fleet out of New York on domestic runs to Miami and Los Angeles, to San Juan, and overseas to Oslo, Brussels, Tel Aviv and Athens.

Focusing more on the cargo business, service to Buenos Aires, Rio de Janeiro and Sao Paolo in South America, and the Trinidadian capital Port Of Spain were all inaugurated with 747F service in 1983, and the same year a new continent, Australia, began receiving scheduled flights via Honolulu to Sydney, Australia. Another addition to the route map was beyond-Europe service to Dhahran in Saudi Arabia, following on from an interline agreement with Saudia Airlines which included a continuation of service onwards to Dubai in the United Arab Emirates.

Further codeshares and interline agreements were created in the same period with Turkish Airlines to interline with their 707 freighters and DC-10 passenger flights at London Heathrow, with Air-India beyond Dubai to Indian cities, and Air Lanka to provide service to the Sri Lankan capital of Colombo and beyond, to connect up to Tiger's Asian terminus in Singapore to create a virtual round-the-world cargo line.

In a major political breakthrough that was the result of years of negotiation, Tiger operated eight charter flights to China in 1984 and forty-one in 1985, mostly carrying livestock and electronics. One wonders what the Chinese authorities thought of this airline, a direct descendant of the air force - it even had the same name - that flew for the other side in the Chinese civil war. Nonetheless, the deal was done and the flights operated, with a third going to Guangzhou and the other two-thirds to Beijing.

1986 saw the addition of Boeing 727-100 freighters for shorter and thinner US flights, and the opening of a massive new Tiger hub at Columbus Ohio's Rickenbacker industrial airport, boasting 196,000 square feet and creating 500 jobs. Every technical in-

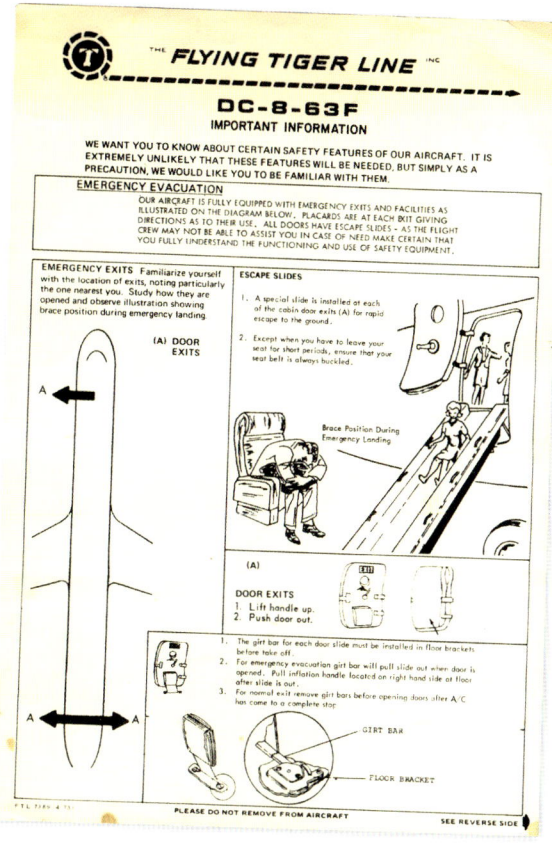

novation that could save even seconds with handling innovations and revisions to operating procedures was applied. Although Tiger was in many ways an old brand, there was no reluctance to embrace new methods or technology.

In the autumn of 1986, ambitious new chairman Stephen M Wolf (who went on to lead United Airlines) and the board put in place a three-point plan: to reduce operating expenses, to reduce and restructure debt, and to implement a strategic plan to ring-fence a defensible niche in the market. The clear focus paid off and in 1987 Tiger posted a $106.6 million profit, and the airline adopted a new motto: "We're taking care of business."

1987 saw Tiger return to the Thai capital of Bangkok for the first time since the end of the Vietnam War, and charter service to Colombo in Sri Lanka was started. New DC-8-73s re-engined with CFM International CFM56 powerplants, a new high-bypass fanjet developed jointly by General Electric in the USA and France's SNECMA, joined the fleet to provide lift on long routes too thin for 747 service, such as Zurich to Charlotte.

In 1988 Europe to Asia links were opened, both via the Persian Gulf (Bangkok to Brussels via Dubai) and via Alaska (Hong Kong to London via Taipei, Seoul and Anchorage).

The good practices and judicious investments of the mid-80s made the legendary company a target for takeover, and on December 17, 1988, Federal Express announced an $880 million buy-out of Flying Tiger Line.

Founded by Frederick W. Smith, Federal Express had started operations on April 17, 1973 with fourteen Dassault Falcon 20 bizjets and an ambitious vision for air freight that involved one carrier being responsible for a piece of cargo from local pick-up all the way to ultimate delivery, operating it's own aircraft, depots and delivery vans, using a single clearinghouse hub, which in practice was Memphis, Tennessee. By 1976 Federal Express was a profitable company with an average volume of 19,000 parcels a day. By 1981 it was competing directly with the US Postal Service express mail, and topped one billion dollars of annual revenue for the first time in 1983. With new hubs at Newark in 1986 and Indianapolis and Oakland in 1988 orbiting the Memphis superhub, international expansion was the next obvious evolutionary step, and Tiger's global operation and it's superb human assets and skills made it the obvious partner.

Saul P Steinberg, Tiger's co-chairman and largest stockholder, granted an option to Federal Express to buy his 14.8% stake, and the parent company, Tiger International, granted the option for Federal Express to buy another 22% in the form of unissued shares. The dual agreements effectively created a lock-out to stop any other company from bidding.

Flying Tigers, with particularly strong international route authorities to Asia, Latin America and Europe was strategically a excellent choice for Federal Express to accelerate its international growth and its global distribution network.

At the time of the acquisition, Tiger flew thirty-nine aircraft including twenty 747s, and employed 6,500 loyal employees. August 7, 1989 was dubbed "T Day" by Federal Express, the day that Tiger officially came into the FedEx family. One by one, Tiger's silver fleet of 747s, DC-8-73s and 727s turned purple with various hybrid liveries incorporating the distinctive Federal Express colours. The DC-8s were never fully painted in the livery of their new owners and disposed of fairly quickly, but several 747s and 727s were fully integrated into the FedEx fleet, which was dominated by DC-10s, 727s of their own.

On June 24, 1994, Federal Express changed its corporate identity to "FedEx". By the end of 1996, all five remaining 747 aircraft in FedEx fleet were transferred to Atlas Air Cargo and progressively replaced by MD-11 and DC-10 equipment. In total twenty-two Boeing 747s were operated by FedEx.

Today, over a quarter of a century later, from the ex-Tiger employees still serving at FedEx to the ranks of retired aviators and employees, every single person involved with the odyssey of the Flying Tiger remembers the "can-do" spirit that began in the early days of World War 2 in the skies over China, then continued at the airfield at Burbank, in the High Tower corporate building next to the runways at LAX, and in cockpits, hangars and freight hubs around the world. The Flying Tiger Line's contribution to opening up the global supply chain of todays' world will never be forgotten.

mostly written at 79 Wardour Street, London - CK

CONGRESSIONAL TRIBUTE TO BOB PRESCOTT

"Robert W. Prescott: a transportation pioneer"

motion brought by Hon. Charles H. Wilson of California in the US House of Representatives
Wednesday March 8, 1978

Mr Speaker, "We'll fly anything, anytime, anywhere." That slogan typified the attitude of a man and the successful company he founded over thirty years ago. Robert W. Prescott, who died Friday from cancer at his home in Palm Springs California, pioneered the air cargo industry in the United States when he founded the Flying Tigers as the first airfreight company in 1945.

As a personal friend of Bob Prescott's, I was constantly amazed at his determination and courage. With little else, he built what has become one of the most successful companies in the business. Today, Flying Tigers is the world's largest all-cargo airline, linking key cities throughout the United States and Asia and covering some 17,500 miles.

Bob Prescott is definitely a model example of the American dream. Starting out with only an idea and heavy competition from hundreds of other war veterans who had the same thought, he convinced some of his old flying buddies and a number of businessmen to invest $178,000 in a new kind of airline — designed specifically for cargo transport.

The name Flying Tigers is familiar to many. It is the popular name given to the famous American Volunteer Group led by General Claire Lee Chennault. The volunteer pilots, one of whom was Bob Prescott, painted snarling jaws filled with sharp teeth on the noses of their P-40 fighters and gave Free China an air defence against the Japanese during World War II. Bob took part in five major campaigns with the Flying Tigers against the Japanese, shooting down six enemy aircraft and finally becoming a Flight Leader.

When the Flying Tigers disbanded in 1942, Prescott returned to this country where he began flying with the Intercontinental Divison of Trans World Airlines. While employed by Trans World, he served as copilot on the plane that took then Ambassador James E. Davies on his famous Mission To Moscow in 1942.

Later than year, he returned to China as a captain with the China National Aviation Corporation, and was assigned to fly military supplies from India to China over the Himalayan mountains. He completed more than three hundred of what became known as the famous "Hump" crossings.

For those of us who knew Bob and certainly based on his flight experience of the early 1940s, it is hardly surprising that he would undertake the task to form the Flying Tiger Line. Starting out with only four airplanes and sixteen employees, he began flying a transcontinental route across the United States — an idea that he sold to the Los Angeles businessmen who helped him raise the initial capital.

After four years of flying, the company finally received official government certification in 1949 and approval for the nation's first commercial all-cargo route — No. 100. Twenty years later, in mid-1969, Bob was able to see his idea receive approval for the first scheduled transpacific all-cargo route that linked its US domestic system with service to eight Asian nations and territories.

In 1970, the airline became a subsidiary of Flying Tiger Corporation, later renamed Tiger International. Prescott was also a director of that corporation as well as the airline and Tiger Leasing Group, another subsidiary of Tiger International, which is engaged in transportation and equipment leasing and financing.

Prescott was born to a large, poor family in Fort Worth Texas, where he tried, for a time, managing prize fighters. Later, he moved to California where he attended Compton Junior College. He then entered Loyola University to study law, but left in 1939 to enlist in the US Navy as an aviation cadet. He was commissioned as an ensign in 1940, and served as flight instructor until he resigned to join General Chennault.

Being the hard-driving chief executive officer for a major company would seem to be enough for anyone. But Bob Prescott was not just anyone. He was also a member of the board of the Transportation Association of America and was a member of the board of directors of the Air Transport Association. Because of his outstanding contributions in the transport field, the National Defense Transportation Association named him "Man Of The Year" in 1973.

Bob was also very active in civic affairs. He was trustee of the City Of Hope, held regional industrial chairmanships in the United Crusade and was an honorary member of the Air Line Pilots Association and the Wings Club of New York. Last year, Northrop

University conferred an honorary Doctor of Science degree on him.

Bob Prescott was a man of personal courage who not only distinguished himself in combat, but in the business world as well. I think his own statement about his accomplishments exemplifies the type of person was. "It is difficult to express the pride I feel at what has happened to a struggling idea I had so many years ago."

Greg Drawbaugh - DrawDecal

2 THE DOUGLAS DC-8

I. THE JOURNEY BEGINS

Donald Wills Douglas was born in Brooklyn, New York, on April 6, 1892. His love of aviation started early, and as a teenager he travelled to Fort Myer in Arlington County, Virginia, to witness the 1908 exhibition flights performed by Orville Wright for the benefit of the US military establishment, the first-ever flights at a US military installation.

The following year Douglas joined the Naval Academy at Annapolis in Maryland, but left in 1912 to study the nascent science of flight, becoming in 1914 the first person to graduate from MIT (Massachusetts Institute of Technology) with a Bachelor of Science in Aeronautical Engineering.

After a brief stint working on dirigible design at the Connecticut Aircraft Company, Douglas joined the Glenn Martin Company in August 1915, making Chief Engineer at the age of 23. When the Glenn Martin Company merged with the Wright Brothers Company in 1916 to form Wright-Martin, Douglas left to become chief engineer for the US Army Signal Corps.

After another brief stint at the reformed Glenn L Martin Company, now in Cleveland Ohio, where he designed the MB-1 bomber, Douglas struck out for pastures fresh in California to form the Davis-Douglas Company with a $40,000 investment from financier David Davis. The intention of the partnership was to build the first aircraft to cross the USA nonstop but the Douglas Cloudster only made it as far as Fort Bliss Texas before it's journey was cut short due to engine failure. However the aircraft did achieve two milestones - it was the first-ever aircraft lift a payload which was greater than it's own empty weight, and set a local Pacific coast altitude record of 19,160 feet. Most significant of all, however: it was the first aircraft to bear the name Douglas.

Following the dissolution of the Davis-Douglas partnership, the Douglas Aircraft Company was formed on July 22, 1921 at the Santa Monica airfield, located at a picturesque spot on the Pacific coast a few miles to the northwest of downtown Los Angeles, California.

The company's first military contract resulted in the delivery of ninety DT (Douglas Torpedo) biplanes, forty-six of which were built at Santa Monica and delivered to the navies of the US, Norway and Peru; twenty more were built under licence by Lowe-Willard-Fowler in New York, six by the Naval Aircraft Factory in Philadelphia, eleven by the Dayton Wright Company, and seven by Marinens Flyvebåtfabrik in Horten, Norway.

The expanding team, which included future aerospace titan John Northrop, created the Douglas World Cruiser (DWC), building five to fly around the world. The four-ship expedition set off from Seattle on April 6, 1924, with two aircraft returning to Seattle joined by the prototype for the final stretch on September 28 after covering 23,942 nautical miles (44,342 km) and averaging seventy miles per hour (113 kmh) for 371 hours and eleven minutes in the air. The success of the DWC put the Douglas Aircraft Company firmly in the big leagues, with a new motto, First Around The World, Around The World First, and a new logo showing three aircraft encircling a globe. This logo would evolve over the decades to include a rocket, and remains Boeing's logo today.

It was the crash of TWA 599 on March 31, 1931 on the first leg of a flight from Kansas City to Los Angeles that stimulated Douglas Aircraft among others to make a great leap forward with airliner technology. The main cause was the failure of the Fokker

F-10 Trimotor's wooden wing whose glue was weakened by moisture. The death toll of two crew and six passengers included beloved Knute Rockne, one of the greatest coaches in American football history. Inadequate hardware had killed before, but the loss of such a well-known figure made the accident a turning point and galvanised the aerospace industry into action.

Boeing were first to respond, with the B-247 which took to the air for the first time on February 8, 1933. Although TWA liked what they saw, their order was rejected because Boeing was also an airline, so no other operator was able to buy the B-247 and the first sixty all went into service, starting on May 22, with Boeing Air Transport (which later became United Airlines). TWA turned instead to Douglas, who after initially doubting the market was big enough to justify the development cost, built a single DC-1 proof-of-concept prototype which first flew from Santa Monica on July 1, 1933 under the control of Captain Carl Cover. The all-metal, low-wing, twin-engined airliner was fully heated, insulated against noise, and was able to takeoff, fly and land on one engine, and even in this embryonic form fully represented the leap forward the airline industry badly needed.

After performing over two-hundred test flights including a cross-country trip in just thirteen hours and five minutes, the DC-1 was handed over to TWA on September 15. The cost of building the aircraft was $325,000 which was immediately justified when TWA placed an order for twenty production models, which were designated DC-2s.

The original DC-1 was sold to Scottish aristocrat Lord Forbes in May 1938, after which it went to Spain and flew for LAPE (Lineas Aereas Postales Espanolas), the Spanish Republican Air Force, and Iberia Airlines, until it force-landed near Malaga in December 1940 and was written off.

The first DC-2 flew on May 11, 1934, and went into service with TWA the following week, May 18. TWA's initial commitment was followed up by orders from KLM, LOT Polish Airlines, Swissair and LAPE; five were built under licence in Japan by Nakajima Aircraft Co, and Douglas also sold sixty-two DC-2s to the US military, bringing production up to a total of one hundred and ninety-eight machines.

However, the DC-2 was merely a warm-up for the DC-3; after a marathon phone call between Donald Douglas and American Airlines CEO CR Smith, Douglas agreed to go ahead with a bigger airliner, based around Smith's desire to replace his fleet of Curtiss Condor IIs with a DC-2 category aircraft that would be wide enough to accommodate sleeping births. Led by engineer Arthur E. Raymond, the Douglas Sleeper Transport (DST) with berths for sixteen, or the DC-3 with seats for twenty-one, emerged and took to the skies over Santa Monica for the first time on December 17, 1935.

The number produced still defies belief to this day - 16,079. The total unpacks as 607 civil DC-3s and 10,048 military C-47s produced either in Santa Monica or at a new plant down the Pacific coastline at Long Beach or at a third production line in Oklahoma City, plus 4,937 in the Soviet Union as the Lisunov Li-2, initially at Aircraft Factory 84 in Khimki just northwest of Moscow, and after the evacuation of Moscow, at the factory of the Tashkent Aviation Production Association (TAPO) in the Uzbek Soviet Republic. A further 487 were built under license as the L2D in Japan by two different airframers, the Nakajimi Aircraft Co and the Showa Corporation.

American Airlines inaugurated service on June 26, 1936; the transformative impact of the DC-3 being so great that this could be considered the founding date of the modern airline industry. By the end of the year KLM was flying scheduled service from Amsterdam to Sydney, which even in 2015 would be the in the top five of the world's longest same-plane air routes.

Even before the DC-3 was in service, Douglas built a single DC-4E, a four-engined tricycle-undercarriage airliner with a triple tail that bore a resemblance to the Lockheed Constellation, in response to a request from United Airlines. First flying on June 7, 1938, the sole DC-4E was put into service by United but proved to be expensive to operate and performance was less than hoped for. The single aircraft was sold to Imperial Japanese Airways, who claimed the aircraft had crashed into Tokyo Bay shortly after delivery, but was in fact used by the Nakajimi Aircraft Co to reverse-engineer the unsuccessful G5N bomber.

However the DC-4E did lead to the better-known DC-4, which shared the four piston engines of it's proof-of-concept predecessor but a simplified empennage. The first production aircraft took to the air on Valentines Day 1942 and 1,163 were built as C-54 transports for the US military to fight World War 2; after the end of hostilities, despite many war-surplus C-54s now available at bargain basement prices, another seventy-nine civilian versions were delivered to airlines including Pan Am, Sabena, Cubana, Iberia, Swissair and Aerolineas Argentinas. In addition, Canadair built seventy-one under licence, known as the North Star, powered by Rolls-Royce Merlin engines and delivered to Trans-Canada Airlines (TCA), the Royal Canadian Air Force (RCAF), Canadian Pacific Airlines (later CP Air) and BOAC (who renamed the aircraft the Argonaut).

During 1940 Douglas built twelve examples of the little-known DC-5, a high-wing transport that was developed from the A-20 Havoc bomber / intruder / night-fighter but overtaken by the global war effort; only longtime Douglas fan KLM (the only airline to operate all Douglas Commercial types from the sole DC-1 onwards) received their machines before the production line was shut down to make more SBD Dauntless dive bombers. Interestingly, the prototype became the personal aircraft of William Boeing, who named it Rover. Other DC-5s had interesting lives, whether it was the damaged and abandoned KLM aircraft that was captured in Indonesia by Japanese forces and later used as a troop transport in Japan, or the three that flew for the USAAF in Australia during the war.

With World War 2 over, Douglas returned to civvie street along with the rest of the nation and launched the DC-6, an evolution of the DC-4 that started life as a military programme called the XC-112 and boasted a stretched fuselage, transatlantic range, and a pressurised passenger cabin. The DC-6 first flew on February 15, 1946 with first deliveries to both American Airlines and United Airlines on November 24. A fatal crash in Utah caused by an in-flight fire on a United flight on October 24 of the following year was followed by a similar conflagration on an American Airlines flight three weeks later; luckily the latter event ended safely with an emergency landing in Gallup, New Mexico. The type was grounded worldwide for four months until the cause was found to be venting fuel which was finding it's way into a cabin heating air scoop; once the design flaw was rectified, the DC-6 went on to become the most successful post-war Douglas airliner, with 538 civilian examples delivered to commercial airlines, plus 101 C-118As for the US Air Force and sixty-five R6D-1s for the US Navy.

American Airlines led the way once more for the last Douglas propliner, the DC-7, essentially a stretched (by forty inches) DC-6 powered by Wright R-3350 turbo-compound engines. 105 standard DC-7s were delivered, all to US carriers, with a first flight of May 18 1953, and entry into service in November the same year. 112 DC-7Bs were built with increased gross weight and extended range, followed by 121 DC-7C Seven Seas, which, as the name suggests, had true long haul capability including nonstop transatlantic range in both directions. The aircraft was a sales hit, ordered in significant numbers by customers throughout the US (including fifty-eight for American Airlines and fifty-seven for United) and Europe (BOAC, Sabena, Swissair, SAS, and KLM among others) as well as further afield (Japan Air Lines, Mexicana, Persian Air Services; South African Airways used the DC-7B to fly all the way from Johannesburg to London with just a single stop), although the Wright R-3350s were troublesome, with diversions due to engine shutdowns. The joke about such-and-such four-engined aircraft being "the best three-engined aircraft ever built" has been applied to many different types but it's true origin is the Wright-powered DC-7 and Super Connie, which would routinely end a trip, either at the destination or at some unplanned intermediate airfield, with a prop feathered.

II. THE JET AGE

The whine of the jet engine was not a novelty in the 1950s, as Maxime Guilliame had patented the idea of using a turbine to power an aircraft as early as 1921, and Alan Arnold Griffith published the ground-breaking An Aerodynamic Theory Of Turbine Design in 1926 for the Royal Aircraft Establishment. Fellow Brit Frank Whittle worked through the 1930s developing axial compressor designs, but the simultaneous efforts of Hans von Ohain in Germany meant the first jet aircraft to fly was the Heinkel He-178 on August 27, 1939. The Messerschmitt Me-262 followed it into the air on July 18, 1942 and ientered service as the world's first operational jet-powered fighter in April 1944. The Brits were right behind, with the Gloster Meteor entering service with the Royal Air Force (RAF) in July of the same year.

With World War 2 still raging, the government of the United Kingdom formed the Brabazon Committee to determine the UK's civil airliner requirements in the post-war phase. Various jet-powered configurations were considered, from small airmail carriers to passenger jetliners, and in December 1945 BOAC ordered ten de Havilland DH 106 Comets. The world's first jet airliner flight was a thirty-one minute sortie in the evening summer sunshine of July 27, 1949 out of Hatfield in the northern suburbs of London, under the command of John "Cat's Eyes" Cunningham (a famous night fighter pilot in World War 2), along with co-pilot Harold "Tubby" Waters, engineers John Wilson (electrics), Frank Reynolds (hydraulics), and test observer Tony Fairbrother. After two years of intense test flying, the first production aircraft, G-ALYP (known as "Yoke Peter" in the phonetic alphabet of the era) first flew on January 9, 1951 and was handed over to BOAC's Comet Unit for test flying, training, and route trials. The world's first jet-powered airline flight took place on May 2, 1952 from London to Johannesburg with five stops en route. By the summer of 1953 BOAC was operating eight jet departures a week out of London - three to Johannesburg, two to Tokyo, two to Singapore, and one to Colombo, all with many stops en route. Rome, Beirut, Basra, Karachi, Rangoon, Cairo, Hong Kong, Hargeisa, Nairobi, Blantyre... Global mass transit was on it's way.

Boeing had made some inroads into the passenger airliner market with the B-377 Stratocruiser (another "best three-engined aircraft ever built") based on the B-29 Superfortress bomber, but only sold fifty-six. The USAF Strategic Air Command (SAC) was in the market for a jet-powered aerial refuelling tanker, and Boeing already had significant jet experience with their B-47 Stratojet which first flew on December 17, 1947. As early as 1950 Boeing were seriously looking at building a jet transport called the Model 473-60C, and by early 1952 started custom-building a one-off proof-of-concept aircraft, which became the Model 367-80, registration N70700. The machine was unveiled in a public roll-out ceremony at the Renton plant on May 15, 1954, and America made a major leap towards the jet age when the "Dash Eighty" took to the air over Washington State on July 15, 1954.

Douglas had created a jet-propelled test aircraft, the XB-43 Jetmaster, as early as 1946, with a first flight date of May 17. The aircraft had stability issues but was an important first step into the jet age for what was then the world's dominant civil airframer. It was followed by another experimental design, the D-558-1 Skystreak. By 1948 Douglas was producing a successful jet fighter aircraft, the F3D Skyknight (265 built), which was eclipsed in 1951 by the supersonic F4D Skyray which sold even more (422) and marked the first time a carrier-based aircraft held the world's absolute speed record of 752.943 mph (1211.74 kph).

Douglas established an office at their Santa Monica plant to study a possible future jet-powered airliner. Chief Project Engineer Ivor Shogrun led a team of designers through the parameters to be massaged: range, payload, number of engines, and cost. Hundreds of configurations were considered, including a delta wing. By mid-1953, a swept-wing design with four podded underwing engines was decided upon, and a full-size wooden mock-up was built to show potential customers. Two versions were proposed: the DC-8A was a domestic machine with a maximum takeoff weight of 209,600 lbs (95,073 kgs) offered for delivery in 1956, while the DC-8B was an overwater variant with a maximum takeoff weight of 248,000 lbs (112,490 kgs) offered for delivery from 1958. Window spacing was governed by a forty-inch pitch (distance between rows of seats), a layout unthinkably spacious for economy seating today; however, the wide window spacing did not change, giving the finished aircraft one of it's signature physical characteristics.

By September 1954, Douglas had committed over $3 million and 250,000 man-hours to the DC-8 project. However, despite the appearance of the 367-80 up in Seattle, Douglas felt the US military would turn to more than one manufacturer for their tanker / transport needs, so a military sale was assured.

May 30, 1958, Long Beach

However, in July 1955, General Curtis LeMay announced an order for twenty-one Boeing KC-135s, the production version of the 367-80. Despite personal appeals by Donald Douglas Sr, the availability of the KC-135 at least a year earlier than an equivalent Douglas product meant SAC had decided to go with an exclusive supplier. (Boeing's invention of the flying air-to-air refuelling boom first deployed on the KC-97 Stratofreighter tanker variant of the B-377 Stratocruiser also helped.) Being the exclusive supplier to the US military in this niche proved to be incredibly lucrative for Boeing, as by the time production ended in 1965, 803 KC-135s were delivered.

Losing the SAC order demonstrated to Douglas that being second in the race had serious commercial consequences. Since a hand-tooled flying prototype would consume valuable time, it was decided that Douglas would go straight to production from Ship One, and the first eight aircraft would be used for flight testing. To reduce surprises, in summer 1955 a complete mock-up was built at a cost of $7.5 million, to establish layout for major items such as ducting, wiring, fuel and hydraulic routing, even the best location for the "black boxes". Accommodating the request from United Airlines for a six-abreast seating layout meant a bigger wing and tail.

The earlier reluctance of Douglas to fully commit to a jet powered transport seemed to be a prudent position to have taken, with the advent of the Lockheed L-188 Electra, Bristol Britannia and Vickers Viscount prop-jets all entering service while the pure jet de Havilland Comet remained grounded after a series of accidents caused by structural failure. The final decision to go ahead with a pure-jet airliner remained with Donald Douglas Sr himself, and it was made on June 7, 1955, with an allocated budget of $450 million, the most expensive privately-financed corporate venture ever, up to that time.

It was ironic that Boeing, by grasping the initiative with the 367-80, had been able to beat Douglas to the punch with the KC-135 order, but Douglas, having acquiesced to United's need for a six-abreast economy seating layout, was able to get the lion's share of the Pan Am order announced on October 13, 1955 - twenty-five DC-8s as opposed to twenty of the five-abreast 707. Because the Pan Am DC-8 order was for the overwater B variant, it was understood that Pan Am would not get the first aircraft built, which would all be domestic A machines, but with that order in the book, the DC-8 was in business.

Following the October 1955 IATA convention in New York, Donald Douglas Sr invited officials from twenty of the world's top airlines to Santa Monica where, on October 25, he and United Airlines president Pat Patterson jointly announced United's order for thirty DC-8As at a cost of $175 million with deliveries beginning in May 1959, the largest single order ever placed for commercial airliners.

National Airlines followed suit on November 7, followed by KLM on November 16. Eastern Airlines president Eddie Rickenbacker announced an order for twenty-six DC-8As at a cost of $165 million in early December, followed by Japan Airlines for four B models to fly transpacific. December 21 saw SAS place an order for seven plus three options. By the time the clocks chimed midnight at the end of 1955, Douglas had orders for ninety-nine DC-8s - a respectable start to paying off their huge investment. The number quickly went into triple figures as Swissair ordered three DC-8Bs on January 30, 1956, followed by Delta for eight DC-8As on February 13. In May 1956 a third DC-8 variant was created for Trans Canada Airlines, who ordered four aircraft to be powered by Rolls-Royce Conway engines, with a total value of $22 million.

The design team were working every bit as hard as the sales team, with extra attention given to noise suppression (a daisy-shaped exhaust system from Rolls-Royce was chosen), braking efficiency (extra airbrakes, later discarded, were added to extend from the fuselage behind the wings), and ground manoeuvring (the main gear would unlock and castor when the nose gear turned more than forty-five degrees). As design work continued, the fuselage kept growing in length, initially to 139 feet six inches, then to 148 feet ten inches, and by the time the design was frozen, 150 feet six inches. Takeoff weight for the DC-8A increased to 265,000 lbs (120,202 kgs) and for the DC-8B to 310,000 lbs (140,614 kgs).

June 1956 saw the important announcement that the DC-8 would be built at Douglas's Long Beach plant, which had seen the creation of 4,285 C-47s (and over 3,000 B-17s under licence from Boeing) during World War 2. The production line would be on a new fifty-five acre plot alongside the existing factory, which by 1956 was being used for the production of the C-133 Cargomaster and B-66 Destroyer light bomber. Completion date for the plant was planned

tive for being blackened by smoke, were picked out by the priest and fashioned into a memorial plaque which is in the chapel to this day.

The early jet age was beset by accidents related to the introduction of the new and demanding technology of jet-powered airliners, which ranged from hydraulic failures (in a single week in October 1960, two United DC-8s and a Western 720 made precautionary landings at Edwards AFB, and a Braniff 707-227 diverted to Carswell AFB near Fort Worth Texas, all due to hydraulic problems), to large-scale disasters such as the 1960 New York Midair Collision. The first nine months of 1961 saw 995 people lose their lives in air disasters (316 in September alone) including sixty-one killed when a jointly operated KLM / Viasa DC-8 crashed into the Atlantic after leaving Lisbon, probably due to instrument failure; and seventeen were killed plus one on the ground in another United DC-8 crash in Denver caused by loss of directional control after landing due to a hydraulic fault.

However, lessons were quickly learned - for instance, in the case of the 1960 New York mid-air collision, although the DC-8 was decelerating rapidly from over 430 knots to prepare for landing, it's speed at the time of impact was still 315 knots; this accident directly led to the 250-knot speed limit below 10,000 feet that remains in place today. The FAA also took action to ensure the highest possible maintenance practices were adhered to, adding inspectors and analysing data to find consistency or patterns of failures. In fact no obvious design faults were found, but experience with the new jets led to the FAA's goal to reduce the incident rate by fifty percent was achieved by April 1962.

DC-8-40, CF-TJD, was handed over to Trans Canada Airlines, and began service after a two-month training period based in Montreal started flying from Montreal to Vancouver via Toronto on April 1, with transatlantic service following on June 1, from Toronto to London via Montreal.

With three more machines on strength by mid-February, Eastern began marketing their new flagship as the DC-8B, which resulted in a lawsuit from National and Delta which Eastern won as such a variant had once existed. (Later, when Pan Am and Northwest Orient began calling their DC-8-30 aircraft "DC-8C", the Civil Aeronautics Board finally called a halt to the escalation and everyone went back to using -10, -20, -30 et al.)

The first European airline to accept delivery of a DC-8 was, aptly, longtime Douglas champion KLM, on March 19. They began service on the Amsterdam to New York run on April 16, which became a daily service ten days later. SAS started Copenhagen to New York with their first DC-8-30 on May 1, and Alitalia's first DC-8-40 started Rome to New York via London on June 1.

The DC-8-12, fitted with the updated wingtips to reduce drag and close in on performance guarantees, was certified on July 12, with previously-delivered DC-8-11s being modified after that date to the new DC-8-12 standard. United subsequently upgraded it's whole fleet of DC-8-12s to become DC-8-21s. Later, a modified leading edge and a four percent chord increase from root to tip was developed to reduce drag at high Mach numbers. Meanwhile aircraft from the test programme were converted back to passenger standard and handed over to their customer airlines, while Ship One stayed in Long Beach to become the prototype fanjet-powered DC-8-50.

Japan Airlines received their first DC-8-32 on July 16, and opened the important route from Tokyo to San Francisco via Honolulu on August 12. French independent carrier TAI (Transports Ariens Intercontinentaux) opened the longest DC-8 route yet on September 4, all the way from Paris to the South Pacific island of Fiji via Los Angeles to join up with Air France's 707 service from Nadi to Paris via the Orient, creating round-the-world jet service for France.

Canadian Pacific's DC-8-43 flights rivalled TAI for length by originating in Amsterdam, flying across the Atlantic, calling in a number of Canadian cities including Montreal, Toronto and Winnipeg, before launching from Vancouver across the Pacific to Honolulu, Auckland and Sydney.

Modifications made in 1960 to active DC-8s included the installation of an extra 950 gallons of fuel capacity in tanks inside the leading edges of Alitalia, SAS and Swissair DC-8-30s to extend range and reduce the number of times westbound transatlantic flights had to call into Shannon or Gander. Pan Am upgraded it's DC-8-32s to DC-8-33 standard by fitting the revised low-drag wingtips, and upgrading the engines to JT4A-11 standard. By the end of 1960, sixteen airlines had taken delivery of 111 DC-8s with a total order book of 156.

However, the year ended in tragedy when United Airlines' N8013U Mainliner Will Rogers collided in cloud over New York with TWA's Super Constellation N6907C Star Of Sicily. Due to a navigation error, the DC-8 was twelve miles off course; after impact, the Connie broke up and dropped onto the northwest corner of Millers Field military airport on Staten Island, while the DC-8, mortally wounded with an engine missing, managed to stay airborne for some time, heading north across the borough of Brooklyn and possibly attempting to reach La Guardia or an off-airport ditching in Prospect Park, but a positive outcome was not to be, and the ship came down in the busy Park Slope neighbourhood, with a total death toll of 134 - six on the ground, forty-four onboard the TWA flight, and eighty-four on the DC-8, including young Stephen Baltz who was found alive in a snowbank at the scene of the crash. Despite the prayers of the whole city, he lost his fight against his injuries at the nearby New York Methodist Hospital the next morning. The small change from the boy's pocket was dropped into the collection box in the hospital's Phillips Chapel by his father, but, distinc-

feet, only 469 knots was being achieved. Ship Two was grounded for a series of wing modifications; a revised wing tip and changes to the shape of the engine exhaust cones went some way to fixing the problem. However there was still a small shortfall and Donald Douglas Sr reduced the price of affected aircraft.

Another unexpected change to the programme was the FAA's announcement that they would only certify the aircraft for a three-person cockpit crew, whereas Douglas had designed the aircraft to be flown by just two crew, with the first officer's seat mounted on tracks and able to slide back to monitor the system panel at critical moments of flight. Canada's Department Of Transport came to the same conclusion, although in their judgement the third person was not initially designated as a flight engineer, but as a third pilot. The DC-8B overwater aircraft were also equipped with a navigator's station.

As plans for more subtypes hit the drawing board, a new and definitive model identification system for the DC-8 was needed, and on February 4, 1960, Douglas vice president of commercial programmes Jackson R. McGowan announced that the domestic version previously known as the DC-8A and powered by JT3C-6 turbojets would become the DC-8-10 (with minor differences of engine power and weights creating the -11 and -12). Domestic DC-8As powered by more powerful JT4A powerplants would become the DC-8-20 (and -21), and the overwater DC-8B, also powered by JT4As, would become the DC-8-30 (and -31, -32, -33, -34). Finally, the DC-8 powered by Rolls-Royce Conways would become the DC-8-40. At the same time, a future variant powered by JT3D turbofans was announced, to become known as the DC-8-50.

Sales appeared gradually as the test programme continued - Northwest Orient ordered five DC-8-30s on December 30, 1958, and Philippine Airlines ordered three in April 1959. In October 1959 Canadian Pacific ordered nine DC-8-40s. United changed it's order from forty DC-8-11s to eighteen, the remaining twenty-two upgraded to DC-8-21 standard.

June 3, 1959 saw the delivery of United's first DC-8-11, Ship Eight N8004U, at a ceremony at the factory in Long Beach. Delta's first DC-8-11 was handed over on July 21. Pilot training with the airlines' new toys took up the next couple of months, while Ship Seven N8068D made an important flight on August 31 from Long Beach to Baltimore to receive the DC-8-11's type certificate a whole month ahead of schedule. The certificate was presented to Donald Douglas Jr on the tarmac at Baltimore Friendship airport by Elwood R. Quesada, chief administrator of the FAA, before N8068D flew on to New York for a major press conference the next day with both United president Pat Patterson and Delta president C. E. Woolman. At the time of certification, the DC-8's order book contained commitments for 143 aircraft by eighteen airlines.

The DC-8 era began on September 18, 1959. Delta were first into the air when DL923 left New York Idlewild (later JFK) at 0920, destination Atlanta; two hours and ten minutes later, United's first DC-8 flight blasted out of San Francisco, destination New York. By the end of 1959, twenty-one DC-8s had rolled off the line at Long Beach, all United or Delta DC-8-11s with the exception of two DC-8-41s for Trans Canada Airlines.

January 3, 1960, saw the first delivery of a DC-8-21 to Eastern Airlines. The new subtype was certified by the FAA on January 19 and Eastern commenced revenue service the very next day with flights between New York and Miami, their signature route.

February 7 must surely have been the busiest day in the history of Douglas operations at Long Beach, starting with the handing over to National Airlines of their first DC-8-21 on February 7 which started passenger flights four days later up against Eastern on the New York to Miami run. Next up was the delivery of the first DC-8-32 to Pan Am, N804PA, the fourth of it's kind off the line; it's three predecessors were still being used in the flight test programme. DC-8 Clipper service was inaugurated from the Pan Am Worldport at New York to Bermuda on March 27, followed by London on April 27. At the end of a very busy day, the first

to be May 1957, but in the event, workers started moving into the sub-assembly area of the plant on February 18. The first wing-to-fuselage mating took place on October 25.

Static testing included the use of a water tank, within which a fuselage section was pressurised and depressurised to simulate airline use, and to check the function of innovative titanium "rip-stoppers" around windows, doors, and all skin cut-outs. The first crack appeared only after 113,000 cycles (takeoffs and landings). The test ended after 140,000 cycles with a prophetic comment from a Douglas engineer: "The very low damage propagation rate after high-time exposure indicates that there will be no rapid deterioration of structure as the DC-8s get old."

An important milestone in the preparation for flight took place on March 26, 1958, when four Pratt & Whitney JT3 engines were attached to Ship One, which was rolled out of the hangar into broad daylight before an invited audience including representatives of all seventeen customer airlines, with Donald Douglas Sr waving from the cockpit windows on one side, and his son, Donald Douglas Jr, now president of the company, waving from the other.

III. THE DC-8 FLIES

May 30 was the big day when DC-8 Ship One N8008D took to the air for the first time, with Arnold G. "Heimie" Heimerdinger at the controls, William "Bill" Magruder in the right seat and Paul Patten at the flight engineer's panel. Flight test engineer Bob Rizer was also onboard, monitoring the flight-data recorders in the main cabin. An escape chute was installed in the lower fuselage in case a rapid inflight evacuation by parachute was necessary, but the two-hour, seven-minute flight went up to 21,000 feet and 350 knots and back without a hitch, accompanied at times by a Cessna T-37 and a United Airlines DC-7 cameraship.

The second flight, two minutes shorter than the first, took place on June 4, and landed at Edwards AFB in the California desert north of Los Angeles. By the end of July, Ship One had performed thirteen flights and logged more than forty-five hours of flight time, and by August 22, seventy-two hours.

Ship Two N8018D first flew on November 29, followed by Ship Three N8028D on December 28 and Ship Four N8038D on January 2, 1959. The first DC-8B, registered N800PA and powered by Pratt & Whitney JT4A engines, joined the test programme on February 20 in full Pan Am livery, followed by two more Pan Am DC-8Bs shortly after. The first Rolls-Royce Conway-powered DC-8, N6577C, first flew on July 23, 1959.

The test programme tested all corners of the flight envelope, going up to 45,000 feet and accelerating to Mach 0.95. On one flight, at 40,000 feet the cabin pressurisation system was shut down to check the cabin for leaks. As well as flying in actual icing conditions, flights were performed with strips of wood attached to wing and tail leading edges to simulate the effect of ice build-up on critical surfaces. Centre-of-gravity checks were done by pumping water between two large tanks, one forward and one aft. A drag-chute was attached to the tail in case help was needed recovering from an unusual attitude in the stalls series, and was designed to reduce speed from 420 knots to 300 knots in just fifteen seconds. The test programme used twenty-six pilots, half of whom had no previous jet experience. The learning curve was steep, but the DC-8 was turning out to be a joy to fly.

Starting on July 24, Ship Seven N8068D's test flights began to wander further afield to simulate real airline flying in demanding places, covering 100,000 miles in six weeks, to places such as Bogota up high in the Andes with an elevation of 8,000 feet, and to Madrid, Montreal, New York, Mexico City and Chicago. The September 3 trip from Long Beach to London on September 3 set a speed record, covering the distance in ten hours, forty-two minutes.

One initial disappointment to come from the test programme was that parasitic drag, caused by friction between the airframe or wing and surrounding airstream, was higher than expected. While the guarantee was a cruising speed of 493 knots at 30,000

On a more positive note, N9604Z, a DC-8-43 destined to become CF-CPG at Canadian Pacific, made history on August 21, 1961, by flying supersonic during a test flight over the Askania Tracking Range near Edwards AFB. This was the first time a commercial airliner exceeded Mach 1, and was not repeated until a Tupolev Tu-144 supersonic airliner broke the speed of sound for the first time on June 5, 1969 (and followed by the Concorde's first trip through the sound barrier on October 1 of the same year). The idea originated with Douglas test pilot Bill Magruder (who later became head of the FAA). The flight was carefully planned, with 5,000 lbs (2,268 kgs) of ballast in the rear cabin to provide an aft centre of gravity to assist with manoeuvrability during the pull-out. N9604Z was accompanied by a Lockheed F-104 Straighter and a two-seat North American F-100 Super Sabre provided by the USAF Flight Test Centre to check speed and atmospheric data for accuracy, which was also corroborated by a weather balloon.

The pilots were Bill Magruder, Paul Patten, Joseph Tomich accompanied by flight test engineer Richard Edwards. The track for the accelerating dive started at the southern tip of Rogers Dry Lake and ended at the southern tip of Rosemond Dry Lake. N9604Z climbed to 52,090 feet (setting an altitude record for an airliner in the process) then, weighing 170,600 lbs (77,383 kgs) of which 31,000 lbs (14,197 kgs) was fuel, pushed over into a fifteen-degree descent with a negative G load of 0.5Gs experienced for the first fifteen seconds. The highest speed achieved was Mach 1.012 at 660.6mph while descending through 41,088 feet, with a maximum true airspeed of 662.5mph achieved at 39,614 feet. Recovery was initiated at 42,000 feet and the aircraft was fully recovered at 36,000 feet with the Mach number back down at 0.95. Maximum G load during the pullout was 1.7Gs. No buffeting was experienced during the transonic period, although some was experienced while decelerating through Mach 0.94 at 35,000 feet, along with a buzzing sensation on the ailerons and rudder tab. CF-CPG, with a small plaque testifying to her place in history on the forward bulkhead, flew for Canadian Pacific right up until retirement and scrapping in 1980 after flying 70,567 hours - the rest all subsonic.

IV. THE ENGINE EVOLVES

The first evolutionary step forward by the DC-8 was the adoption by Pratt & Whitney of the turbofan, which is the addition of a first stage ducted fan to the front of a turbojet, with some or much of the airflow bypassing the jet engine core. The first turbofan should have been the result of work by Russian designer Arkhip Lyulka but the Nazi invasion of the Soviet Union during World War 2 meant that his prototypes had to be abandoned in the mass evacuation to the Ural Mountains in 1941. The Rolls-Royce Conway as fitted to the DC-8-40 (as well as the Vickers VC-10 and Boeing 707-420) was the world's first turbofan engine to go into production but had a very low bypass ratio of 0.3.

Pratt & Whitney swapped the first three stages of the eight stage JT3C turbojet's LP compressor with a ducted two stage fan to create the JT3D, one of the most successful early jet engines ever built, with around 8,600 produced and also used to power the Boeing 707-320 and B-52H Stratofortress, as well as the Lockheed C-141 Starlifter military strategic airlifter.

DC-8-63 maiden flight on April 10, 1967

To fit Pratt & Whitney's turbofan to the DC-8, Douglas redesigned the engine pylon, pod, and reverse thrust system, which was moved aft of the hot section and used a series of slots and cascades to redirect exhaust gases forward. With the engine much quieter than it's predecessor, the daisy petal sound suppressor was also dispensed with. Ship One, still in use as a test aircraft by Douglas and based at Long Beach, was first to have the new modifications and performed it's first flight as a DC-8-50 on December 20, 1960, with Heimie Heimerdinger in command.

The first production series 50, a -53 for KLM, was handed over on April 3, 1961. The additional thrust and reduced fuel consumption made the DC-8-50 an easy choice for new and existing customers, and at the time of the handover, DC-8-50s had been ordered by Trans Caribbean Airlines, National Airlines, United Airlines, Philippines, Iberia and Aeronaves de Mexico, some of which were ordered as -30s and upgraded before manufacture.

On April 21, PH-DCP, KLM's second DC-8-53, established a distance record by flying from Long Beach to Rome in eleven hours and seventeen minutes, before continuing to Amsterdam then back across the Atlantic to Caracas and back to Long Beach as part of an FAA reliability and functionality test. The type certificate was duly awarded a few days later, on April 28, 1961.

Ship One, having finished certifying the series -50, was finally of no further use to Douglas and sold to charter carrier Trans International Airlines (TIA; later Trans America Airlines or TAA) at the end of 1960. It was leased it to Lufthansa in 1965 for additional transatlantic lift in full Lufty colours but still sporting it's original N8008D registration; and was later leased to Canadian Pacific as CF-CPN. Delta Airlines bought it on October 1, 1967 and flew it for ten years on US trunk routes as N8008D once more. FB Ayer bought the historic aircraft on March 23, 1979 and leased it to AeroMexico where it flew for the next three years as XA-DOE, then subleased it to TAC Colombia. Ship One was parked in Marana, Arizona in January 1982, where, with 60,918 hours and 32,411 flights in the log book, it was finally scrapped in 2001.

On February 20, 1962, Ship 155 N9608Z Pacific Pacer was used to complete another long distance flight to show the capability of the aircraft, by flying from Seattle to Tokyo with a 41,005 lb (18,600 kgs) payload. The return flight beat the trip to Rome in distance with an eye-watering 8,792 mile sector all the way from Tokyo to Miami, completed in thirteen hours and fifty-two minutes. (Boeing had flown a 707 7,023 miles from Seattle to Beirut earlier the same month, so the Long Beach vs. Seattle rivalry was clearly alive and well.)

Also in February 1962, Douglas were able to demonstrate complete automatic landing capability with an upgraded Sperry SP-30 automatic flight control system; previous incarnations only permitted "hands off" approaches to the middle marker.

The subtype designation DC-8A was revived in the early 1960s for a cargo variant with a swing tail, side cargo door and strengthened floor, and also had the marketing name of Jetmaster and, for the US military, the model number 1920. In May 1961 the type was redesignated the DC-8-50CF (convertable freighter) Jet Trader, initially with a fixed bulkhead that allocated the forward two-thirds of the cabin to cargo; the swing tail option was later discarded and the partition become moveable.

By September the Jet Trader design had evolved, including the rearward repositioning of the aft pressure bulkhead by seventy-nine inches and it's redesign from a dome to a flat panel, which conserved space and enlarged the cabin. Despite an increase in maximum takeoff weight to 315,000 lbs (142,882 kgs) and a new maximum landing weight of 224,000 lbs (101,615 kgs), the application of beefed-up landing gear, new brakes with enhanced anti-skid units, and a more muscular ground spoiler configuration made the landing distance shorter than on previous DC-8s by more than 1,000 feet (305 metres).

The only buyer of the all-cargo windowless DC-8-50 Jet Trader was United, with an order for fifteen, who dubbed them DC-8-54CJ-AF (for "All Freight"). Douglas also produced a number of other oddball -50s. Since the -50 shared the same external dimensions as the -30, KLM, Garuda Indonesia and Japan Airlines liked the performance and enhancements of the -50 but wanted interior commonality with their -30s, giving rise to the -55L, which stood for "Less Bulkhead" and had the original dome-shaped aft pressure bulkhead and resulting shorter interior cabin dimension. While this degree of customisation was greatly appreciated by buyers, it would lead the company into series financial difficulty by incurring significant additional production costs. (A variation cited as being the epitome of paperwork and cost headaches was the number of shades of white paint offered, which apparently numbered more than thirty.)

Orders picked up with commitments from Canadian Pacific for Jet Traders to replace their CL-44 propliners, plus new orders from Trans International, Trans Caribbean, and top-ups from Alitalia, KLM, Delta, Japan Airlines and Swissair, Capitol and a new customer, who ordered a pair of Jet Traders: Flying Tiger Line.

Trans Canada Airlines made history with a Jet Trader by operating the first-ever combi (mixed passenger and cargo configuration on the main deck) flight with the departure of a new service from Montreal to London via Prestwick on the evening of March 2, 1963 operated by CF-TJL with 117 seats and four freight pallets on the main deck.

A Trans International Jet Trader carried a record payload of 87,000 lbs (39,463 kgs) from Travis AFB to Saigon on May 22, 1963 (with fuel stops en route). Swissair stretched the legs of their first Jet Trader by flying it 7,460 miles (12,006 kms) from Long Beach all the way to Beirut in October. By the end of the year, total DC-8 deliveries had reached 192, with twenty-four orders outstanding.

N779FT on the production line

Although Douglas felt the DC-8 was good for about twenty-five aircraft a year, sales slumped in 1964 with only fourteen orders booked for the entire year, nine of which were for United. This left the company with no option but another evolutionary leap forward.

V. THE DC-8 GROWS UP

Douglas had been considering a major stretch of the DC-8 for trunk routes such as California to Hawaii and New York to Puerto Rico. The basic platform was much easier to stretch due to it's high landing gear compared to the 707, which rode considerably closer to the runway and the DC-8's modest wing sweep meant engine pods would not risk scraping the ground during takeoff and landing. The DC-8-61 was the first stretched model, with a 200 inch (five metre) plug inserted ahead of the wing and another 240 inches (six metres) inserted behind the wing, resulting in a new fuselage length of 187 feet four inches (fifty-seven metres). Some of the additional structural weight was offset by an aggressive weight-saving programme which found 2,000 lbs (907 kgs) of savings, mostly by replacing non-loadbearing metal parts with plastic.

The new DC-8-61 was able to accommodate 269 passengers in seating that was compatible with any other type of airline seating using twin tracks along the floor (earlier DC-8s required bespoke seating that attached to the cabin wall). The cockpit instrumentation and lighting borrowed from the new Douglas shortfall DC-9 twinjet. The wing and engines were retained from the DC-8-55, making this, despite it's impressive new dimensions, a "minimum change" upgrade.

Douglas then turned their attention to upgrading the wing and engines. The main focus was initially the engine pods; the reverse-thrust mechanism was changed from three units to one, and the heat exchangers were relocated from the pod to the pylon which reduced the pod's maximum diameter by twelve percent. A three-foot wing tip extension along with new leading edge tanks increased fuel capacity by 900 gallons. With a lesser stretch of eighty inches (two metres) of the DC-8-55 and the incorporation of these aerodynamic enhancements, the DC-8-62 was a true ultra-longranger, able to fly 6,000 miles (9,656 km) with a load of 189 passengers using the unchanged exit configuration from the DC-8-55.

The final upgrade was to marry the -61 fuselage stretch to the -62 wing and engines, to create the world-beating DC-8-63, which would eventually account for a fifth of all DC-8 sales.

The three variants of the Series Sixty DC-8 were launched on April 4, 1965, with an initial order from SAS for four DC-8-62s with four options, followed by United Airlines for five DC-8-61s (and a top-up of various -50s) and Eastern Airlines for eight -61s. By the end of 1965, Douglas had orders for thirty-eight Series Sixtys as well as thirty-six -50s including twelve Jet Traders, although cashflow problems that were a nuisance when orders were scarce was now a crisis with the pick-up of the DC-8 and a boom in orders for the DC-9. The earlier decision to build both the DC-8 and DC-9 on the same production line had to be reversed as orders poured in, creating two separate production lines; this reorganisation alone ate up precious capital.

The first DC-8-61, N8070U, rolled off the line at Long Beach on January 26, 1966, and took to the air for the first time on March 14 in the capable hands of Don Mullin and Heimie Heimerdinger, along with flight engineers Joe Tomich and Richard Edwards. The flight commencing with a takeoff at a gross weight of 255,000 lbs (115,666 kgs), left the ground at a speed of 137 knots and climbed to 31,000 feet. The aircraft then descended towards Palmdale airport north of Los Angeles where a number of touch-and-go landings were flown without a full-stop landing, before returning to Long Beach four hours and forty-five minutes later.

The Port Authority of New York had some concerns about noise from the new stretched DC-8s which proved to be groundless, but they also pointed out that the DC-8-63 would exceed the bearing limits of 430psi on runways and taxiways at John F Kennedy airport. This was received early enough that Douglas was able to revise the main landing gear footprint by moving the wheels 31.25 inches (79.38 cm) apart, as opposed to thirty inches (76.2 cm) on the older DC-8s, which expanded the tyre contact area from 200 square inches to 220 square inches.

A long-range test flight by N8070U operated on August 16 from Long Beach to Tokyo in eleven hours and fifty minutes, followed by twenty-four hours on the ground for Japan Airlines executives and technicians to inspect the new machine. The return to North America was operated from Tokyo to Winnipeg in Manitoba in just eleven hours. After 124 test flights totalling 175 hours in the sky, the DC-8-61 was issued with it's type certificate on September 1, 1966.

The first DC-8-62 took to the air for the first time on August 29 with Paul Patten in command, Don Mullin in the right seat, and Steve Benya on the flight engineer's panel, as well as two test technicians in the cabin.

With the new Series Sixty DC-8s as well as the shorthaul DC-9 available, the Douglas sales team were booking record numbers of orders but with Douglas' persistent cashflow problems, things got worse, rather than better. Deliveries fell woefully behind schedule, with United asking Douglas to paint a test aircraft in United livery so at least publicity photographs would give the illusion that the airline's new flagship was close to delivery even if reality was somewhat less appealing. The Vietnam War was adding to the difficulties of the commercial division, as the national war effort sucked up manpower and physical resources.

The state of distress at Douglas was widely known and merger partners circled, including North American, Martin Marietta, General Dynamics, Fairchild Aircraft and Signal Oil. The decision to merge with McDonnell Aircraft Corporation of Saint Louis, Missouri, was announced on January 13, 1967.

With the merger announcement still in the headlines, United finally received their first DC-8-61 on January 26, 1967 and inaugurated service on the busy Los Angeles to Honolulu run on February 25; Eastern Airlines opened DC-8-61PF service between New York and San Juan on March 3.

The first DC-8-63, N1503U, was rolled out on March 6 and first flew on April 10, another five hour sortie, this time with Cliff Stout and Harry Terrell flying. Meanwhile the DC-8-62 was certified on April 27, and the first example delivered to SAS on May 3. Entry into service followed on the Copenhagen to New York route on May 22. The DC-8-63 followed a similar pattern by being certified on June 29, the first machine delivered to KLM on July 15, and put into service on the North Atlantic on July 27.

Flight testing in 1968 focused on getting the freight versions of the Series Sixty range certified; the DC-8-63CF first flew on March 16 and was certified on June 10; Seaboard World received the first of the type and immediately put it into service on trips to Asia in support of the Vietnam War.

Flying Tigers had ordered nineteen of the DC-8-63 and the first ship was delivered in the first week of July 1968. Early problems in Tiger service with poor braking effectiveness on wet runways resulted in a trial by McDonnell Douglas at their test facility at Yuma, Arizona, on a flooded runway. Serious hydroplaning resulted just as Tiger predicted, and sufficient improvements were made to the Hydrol Mark II antiskid braking system that it was rebranded the Mark III and fitted to all DC-8-63s. The final variant of the DC-8 was the -63AF, and the first of it's kind was delivered to Tiger on October 18. The airline was so thrilled with the productivity of the aircraft that they publicly announced that each airframe would pay for itself in just twelve months, based on an acquisition price of eleven million dollars and each flight grossing $53,000 on a schedule of sixteen round trips per month.

1968 saw the very last DC-8-50s roll off the line - the last passenger aircraft went to Air Canada on October 16, and the last freighter to United on November 23. Total production of standard DC-8s (series -10,

-20, -30, -40 and -50) came to 294 aircraft, including thirty-nine convertibles and United's oddball fifteen windowless DC-8-54AF freighters.

Total deliveries for 1969 numbered a record 101, which was doubly impressive given that the production line was physically small considering the size of the aircraft and the numbers being built, and much of the work was done outside on the flight line.

VI. SUNSET FOR THE DIESEL EIGHT

With the widebody DC-10 and Lockheed L-1011 peoplemovers coming, sales for the narrowbody DC-8, which had always come in volatile peaks and troughs, were winding down for the last time. However, 1969, the last year of DC-8 sales, included the wooing of four new customers - World Airways, American Flyers Airline, West German leisure carrier Air Atlantis, and Air Zaire. Existing operators put their hat in the ring one last time - Airlift, Braniff, and Japan Airlines all placed top-up orders. The last order to be placed was by SAS in April 1971 for a final DC-8-63.

Production was slowly reduced, from 1968's high watermark to eighty-five in 1969 to thirty-three in 1970, twelve in 1971, and a final four aircraft were built in 1972; SAS got their last -63 on May 17, and with it, production of the first Douglas jetliner came to an end. It wasn't quite the sad occasion it might have seemed, as McDonnell Douglas were keen to free up the production space to build the widebody DC-10 which went on to outsell the competing Lockheed L-1011 Tristar by nearly 2:1.

Despite revenue generated by DC-8 sales exceeding $4.5 million, it is hard to say if the programme truly made a profit for Douglas due to the high development costs of so many variants, and the production costs of endless customisation for different airlines. The residual income generated by spares sales and product support certainly added to the bottom line for decades after the end of production.

The DC-8 was present on the airways with the early standard -10, -20, -30 and -40 series, in the early part of the jet age when flying was reserved for the megarich, movie stars, captains of industry, diplomats and spies, with hand-written paper tickets, boarding and deplaning by stairs, uncertain safety records even aboard household-name airline brands. The advent of the fan-powered -50 opened up the airways towards the end of the decade alongside the 707-320 with fares starting to come down. And although the Series Sixty machines were a product of the 1960s, it was in the 1970s they dominated, becoming trunk liners in an era when air travel started to look like it does today, with reservations handled by computer for the first time, boarding by airbridge, fares down and passenger numbers way up. No longer did every man wear a tie, and nor did every lady wear hat and gloves. The great human migration by air had begun in earnest.

The 1970s also saw some aircraft find their way to the second-hand market, and to new homes at airlines such as Loftleidir, providing cheap transatlantic passenger flights via it's home base in Iceland. Second tier North American carriers such as Canada's Nationair, Ontario Worldair, and Quebecair, Air Bahama, Cayman Airways, and Air Jamaica snapped up spare DC-8s for transatlantic trips and winter vacation flights to the Caribbean. Other second-hand frames began migrating to Africa, to carriers such as TAAG Angola and Air Zambia.

European leisure carriers fell in love with DC-8s across the continent; major operators of second-hand aircraft included SATA and Balair (both Switzerland), Spantax, Air Spain, TAE, Canafrica (all Spain), Sudflug (Germany), Sterling (Denmark), Birgenair (Turkey), Point (France), Martinair (Holland), and Pomair Ostend (Belgium) all operated DC-8s, and some of Iberia's machines migrated to Spanish domestic carrier Aviaco for use as peoplemovers in the heavily-travelled Spanish domestic market, including Madrid to Barcelona, the world's busiest domestic air route.

In 1972, an aftermarket "wide body" interior upgrade was offered to DC-8 operators by Heath Technica Corporation of Kent in Washington State, and installed by United Airlines, starting with their own aircraft. The same year, Douglas also offered a wide body interior upgrade. Both offered a lower, rounded ceiling, new side walls and window frames, pull-down blinds to replace old-fashioned curtains, and enclosed overhead bins to replace open hat racks. Japan Airlines was a eager adopter of the new-look interiors and did conversions themselves at Tokyo's Haneda airport using kits made under licence from Douglas by Atlantic Aviation.

As the 1970s moved on, airlines who were ready to upgrade from DC-8s to newer hardware in the sold their aircraft for as little as half a million dollars (in the case of older -20s and -30s), even though the airframes still had a few decades of life left in them. As a result, cheaply acquired older DC-8s began to be converted to freighters starting in 1974 by Charlotte Aircraft Corporation, especially Jet Traders which already had main deck side cargo doors. Modifications involved only the strengthening of floors, installation of roller loading systems, and the replacement of window panes with sheet metal blanks. Main deck side cargo doors were relatively easy to add. At least twenty-five DC-8-30s were modified to DC-8-30Fs by Charlotte Aerospace, and even nine early-build -10s and -20s.

Demand for DC-8 freighter conversions became so great that Douglas opened a production line in March 1976 at it's facility in Tulsa, Oklahoma. Modifications included upgrading old -10s, -20s and -30s to -50 standard by fitting Pratt & Whitney JT3D turbofans and the accompanying newer pylons. Even two Rolls-Royce Conway powered -43s were converted to -43Fs and ended up at AeroPeru, and three other -43s were refitted with Pratt & Whitney JT3Ds, to make them -54Fs; these aircraft went to Zantop and Airlift.

UTA Industries in Paris (a highly capable aerospace spin-off of UTA / Aeromaritime Airlines who later built two Supper Guppy Turbine super transporters for Airbus out of kits supplied by Aero Spacelines among other achievements) converted two -33s to -54Fs for the French Air Force, and Aeronavali in Italy also did some conversions.

Later, passenger Series Sixty and Series Seventy DC-8s began conversion to freighters, also by Aeronavali, on behalf of customers such as Air Canada, UPS (with thirteen ex-Delta passenger liners, the last of which flew in service on May 1, 1989 from Baltimore-Washington to Atlanta), and Guinness-Peat Aviation (with all twenty-nine ex-United -71s).

VII. A LAST HURRAH

Despite the type's continuing popularity with many passenger carriers and a growing fan club in the air cargo business, a dual threat began to loom over the first generation jetliners towards the end of the 70s, in the form of increasingly stringent noise regulations, and with the increase of fuel prices, efficiency. Incredibly, an early consideration was to re-engine DC-8s with General Electric CF-6 engines as found on the widebody DC-10 and Boeing 747; such an excess of power would have surely made the one-off trip through the sound barrier for that Canadian Pacific DC-8-40 back in August 1961 a routine affair. General Electric also had meetings with airlines as early as July 1975 about their planned CFM-56 turbofan, but the form of future noise regulations was too vague to take expensive action, especially on an as-yet-unproven engine.

In 1977, retired Douglas executive Jackson R McGowan formed a new company along with other former top brass from the company to contract for any type of DC-8 retrofit projects, and named it Cammacorp. The new outfit returned to General Electric to discuss the CFM-56, which GE was producing in cooperation with SNECMA (Societe Nationale d'Etude et de Construction de Moteurs d'Aviation). McDonnell Douglas weren't incredibly thrilled by the development, trying as they were to sell new DC-10s, an enterprise already hampered by a perceived safety crisis after a series of public and deadly crashes.

In May 1978, Delta Airlines was the first carrier to seriously consider re-engining it's fleet of DC-8s, as there was no replacement aircraft type that could perform the same missions with the same payload (a problem that plagued all DC-8 operators to some extent!).

Pratt & Whitney offered a competing re-engine programme based around their new JT8D engine in early 1979 which was being developed for the DC-9-80 (later rebranded the MD-80) and this was initially an early favourite with United (an order was actually announced on March 29, 1979), partly due to it's lower purchase price ($980,000 per JT8D compared to $1.5 million for a CFM-56), but it was Flying Tigers who convinced United to take a second look at the CFM offering. Tiger's concern was that the Pratt & Whitney product would offer less thrust in a noise-abatement departure climb, and also calculated that the additional fuel efficiency of the higher-bypass CFM would soon offset the higher purchase price.

In mid April Tiger went ahead and announced that it had contracted with Cammacorp to convert it's nine owned DC-8 Series 60s (seven -63CF and two -61CF machines). Delta followed with a deal for upgrades to thirteen DC-8-61s and soon McGowan had orders for seventy-eight coversions from seven airlines, worth $12 million per aircraft.

Cammacorp struck a deal with McDonnell Douglas in Long Beach to provide all engineering support, and their facility in Tulsa to do the actual conversions; and in May 1979 Grumman Aerospace was lined up to manufacture the engine nacelles and pylons. The first aircraft to be converted was N8093U, a United DC-8-61 that was delivered to Tulsa in October 1980. At this point it was announced that re-engined -61s would become DC-8-71s, re-engined -62s would become DC-8-72s, and re-engined -63s would become DC-8-73s.

More customers for re-engining came through during 1981 including Cargolux, Air Canada, Overseas National Airways and Capitol Airways. Spantax placed an order but went out of business before completion. Flying Tiger convinced the owners of their nine leased DC-8s to do the conversion, five of which belonged to Transamerica Corporation. The first Tiger DC-8-63 arrived in Tulsa in April 1981. Delta took a unusual route, by getting the first of nineteen done at Tulsa then performing the rest themselves in the hangar at Atlanta.

FAA certification for the DC-8-71 was granted on April 13, 1981, with certificates for the -72 and -73 following in May. Delta put their first -71 into service from Atlanta to Savannah on April 24, followed by United from San Francisco to Portland Oregon on May 16. Transamerica was first to fly the -73 in revenue service, on a long haul trip from Oakland to Shannon with 254 passengers aboard.

Despite the already healthy order book, Cammacorp continued looking for new business opportunities and to that end, demonstrated the almost unlimited capabilities of the re-engined DC-8 Series Seventy by flying their DC-8-72 test and demonstration machine from Cairo to Los Angeles in fifteen hours and forty-six minutes on April 3, 1983 with former Douglas test pilot Don Mullin in command. (On arrival, the aircraft had enough fuel to fly for another 1,000 miles.) UPS, German Cargo and Emery Worldwide signed up to have their DC-8s re-engined.

An extension of the implementation of FAR Stage 2 noise restrictions from 1983 to January 1, 1986 reduced the urgency felt by airlines, and the availability of cheaper hush kits for JT3D-powered aircraft took some of the bite out of Cammacorp's sales presentations, and with the march of time, there were fewer and fewer remaining airframes suitable for conversion. In mid-1986 Cammacorp began winding down their operation, although they also pioneered the addition of digital, or glass cockpit technology to the DC-8 in partnership with Honeywell and Collins Aerospace.

Remaining DC-8s not re-engined still had to comply with FAR 36 Part 2 noise regulations however, and the market responded by making more hush kits available, such as the DyanRohr package supplied by Rohr Industries under contract to Jersey (United Kingdom) based Aeronautic Development Corporation who built and sold fifty shipsets, or the Quiet Nacelle Corporation of Waco Texas who sold another twenty-eight of a competing design. Other hushkit options were provided by Snow Aviation (supplied to Worldways Canada), Burbank Aeronautical Corporation (supplied to Airborne Express), and UAS Engineering.

In May 1988, a highly symbolic torch was passed, when Douglas announced that it had sold the rights to manufacture spare parts for all Douglas Commercial aircraft from the DC-3 to the DC-8 to Gulfstream Aerospace. This allowed Gulfstream, at its Oklahoma City factory, to fabricate any part or tooling using technical data supplied by Douglas, which for many years fully occupied a team of over 200 staff.

At the time of writing, there are only a tiny handful of DC-8s left flying in the world - a couple of VIP machines, a couple of freighters (mostly at Agro Air in Sri Lanka) and the NASA flying laboratory detailed below. The last active DC-8 simulator has been decommissioned, making training harder (usually requiring the use of an actual aircraft to pound the circuit). Parts are harder to come by, as retired aircraft parked in the desert that would traditionally have been used as Christmas trees for spares have been scrapped over the years due to low demand.

The DC-8 brought many airlines and millions of passengers into the jet age and revolutionised the air cargo industry. It's impact on the world aviation scene is forever, and for now, still, there is a Diesel Eight in the air every day somewhere in the world 2015, flying on the wings of a heritage that stretches back to the century before last, to the birth of its creator, Donald Douglas Sr, in 1892.

mostly written at the Westin St Francis Hotel, San Francisco; with a nod of gratitude to Sophie Thompson onboard N649UA, London to Chicago, March 26 2015: "even the most implausible dream seems realistic when you're dreaming it" - CK

3 HAPPY TIGER RECORDS

An unusual side project for the Flying Tiger Line was to found a record label, called Happy Tiger Records, in 1969. The music industry can be a cash sinkhole for music fans with some money to invest, but Happy Tiger defied the stereotype and proved to be a reasonably successful venture and in it's three years of existence released twenty-seven albums as well as numerous singles. The offices were initially located at 1801 Avenue Of The Stars in Century City, near downtown Los Angeles and later at 6585 Sunset Boulevard in Hollywood.

The catalogue included two albums by Them (after the departure of Van Morrison), two Mason Proffit albums, and a Count Basie album among other things. The label won critical acclaim for it's compilation of Chicago blues recordings originally made by Dunwich / Destination Records. A co-venture with Era Records saw the release of several reissues including some early Beach Boys recordings originally made by producer Hite Morgan. The label closed in 1971.

The full catalogue including joint ventures with Era Records:

Artist	Title	Catalogue #
Buddy Bohn	Places	HTR-1001
Priscilla Paris	Priscilla Loves Billy	HTR-1002
Red Rhodes and The Detours	Live at the Palamino	HTR-1003
Them	Them	HTR-1004
Dan Terry	Lonely Place	HTR-1005
The Kimberlys	The Kimberlys	HTR-1006
Count Basie	Basie on the Beatles	HTR-1007
Ecology	Environment/Evolution/Ecology	HTR-1008
Mason Proffit	Wanted	HTR-1009
Aorta	Aorta 2	HTR-1010
Hal Rugg	Steals the Hits of Loretta Lynn	HTR-1011
Them	Them in Reality	HTR-1012
The Kimberlys	New Horizon	HTR-1014
Paul Kelly	Stealin' in the Name of the Lord	HTR-1015
Anita Kerr Singers	A Tribute to Simon and Garfunkel	HTR-1016
Various	Early Chicago, Volume 1	HTR-1017
Buffalo Nickel Jug Band	Buffalo Nickel Jug Band	HTR-1018
Mason Proffit	Movin' Toward Happiness	HTR-1019
Phil Baugh	California Guitar	HTE-801
Herb Newman	Herb Newman presents AM-FM	HTE-803
various artists	Rare Records Revisited	HTE-804
Beach Boys	Biggest Beach Hits	HTE-805
various artists	Rock n Roll Jukebox	HTE-806
various artists	Golden Era Series, volume 1	EGS-VOL-1
various artists	Golden Era Series, volume 2	EGS-VOL-2
various artists	Golden Era Series, volume 3	ES-VOL-3
Dorsey Burnette	Greatest Hits	ES-800

4 INDIVIDUAL AIRCRAFT LIST

This list has been compiled with information extracted from Servaas C. Verbrugge's DC-8 production list available on his airlinerlist.com web site, supplemented and collaborated by other information including the DC-8 production list by Lundkvist Aviation Research.

Each DC-8 aircraft history is listed in two parts:
1. by factory deliveries to Flying Tiger Line
2. then by DC-8 aircraft either bought or leased to Flying Tiger Line on the used aircraft market.

The heading for each airframe denotes manufacturer's serial number (MSN); and line number.

The history of each individual aircraft then follows in aircraft type order.

Standard abbreviations are incorporated to conserve space. The following most common are:

AL	Airlines
AW	Airways
brup	broken up
canc	cancelled
col	colors
cvtd	converted
cs	color scheme
dam	damaged
del	delivered
eng	engines
fc	full colors
frd	ferried
Id	identity
Int'l	International
i/s	in service
lsd	leased
nn	new name/renamed
nr	near
NTU	not taken up
oc	old colours
opf	operated for
own	owned by
pwfu	permanently withdrawn from use, retired
pkd	parked
rgd/r	registered
s	seen
sis	seen in service
slsd	sub-leased
str	stored
svcs	Services
repo	repossessed
rr	re-registered
rt/ret	returned
tit	titles
TT	total time (flying hours)
wfu	withdrawn from use
W/O	written off by accident

45818/242 — N802SW
55CF Jet Trader — mfd 26.10.1965

N802SW Flying Tiger Line del 13.11.65; Seaboard World AL lsd 13.11.65; Douglas slsd 22.01.69; Seaboard ret 02.04.69, own International Aerodyne 17.10.69; Int'l Air Bahama slsd 17.10.69; repainted at MIA 19.10.69; Seaboard ret 21.05.70; Trans Mediterranean AW slsd 21.05.70; seen LHR 05.06.70 still in ex Int'l Air Bahama cs; Seaboard ret 01.05.71; **TF-LLK** Loftleidir Icelandic slsd 01.10.71 and named "Leifur Eiriksson"; **N802SW** Seaboard World AL ret 16.09.73; **PH-MBH** Martinair Holland 21.09.73; Garuda lsd 01.12.74 with Garuda sticker; cr on approach 04.12.74 nr Colombo, Sri Lanka; TT 42.830h.

Accident description
The flight is said to have departed Surabaya, Indonesia at approximately 12.03 UTC heading to Jeddah planning a stop at Bandaranayake airport, Colombo, Sri Lanka. At around 16.30 UTC Colombo control cleared the flight. At 16.38 UTC another air traffic controller is said to have intervened and cleared the flight down to 5000 feet and reported clearing to 8000 feet. Colombo approach then cleared the flight down to 2000 feet at 16.44 and told the flight to expect a runway 04 approach. The crew aboard the flight were then asked to report when the airfield was in sight. The crew then continued their descent until the aircraft crashed into Saptha Kanya Mountain at an altitude of approximately 4,355 feet and at around 40 nm east of Colombo. All 191 passengers and crew were killed. The crash remains the worst in Sri Lankan aviation history and the third-deadliest involving a DC-8, after Arrow Air Flight 1285 and Nigeria Airways Flight 2120.
PROBABLE CAUSE: "Collision with rising terrain as the crew descended the aircraft below safe altitude owing to incorrect identification of their position vis-a-vis the airport. The investigation is of the opinion that this was the result of dependence on Doppler and Weather Radar Systems on board PH-MBH which left room for misinterpretation."

N802SW — Air Bahama — 1969 — Brussels

N802SW ▰ *1971* ▰ in ex International Air Bahama livery Coll. Guy Van Herbruggen

PH-MBH ▰ *Martinair Holland* ▰ *1973* ▰ *Los Angeles*

45

45821/255   N803SW
55CF Jet Trader   mfd 16.02.1966

N803SW Flying Tiger Line del 17.03.66; Seaboard World AL ntu; Seaboard World AL lsd 18.03.66; own International Aerodyne 03.11.69; Universal AL slsd 21.11.69; Seaboard ret 21.03.70; Japan AL slsd 01.04.70 in full JAL c/s; Seaboard ret 31.03.72; International Aerodyne ret 08.10.72; **TR-LQR** Affretair 09.10.72 named "Situtunga"; **A40-PA** Cargoman lsd 20.01.77; **VP-WMJ** Affretair ret 06.82; seen at LGW 04.06.82, named "Capt. Stock Wallek"; **Z-WMJ** Affretair rr 11.83; **EL-KRU** Liberia World AW 11.97; s16.02.98 Ostend silver, blue tail; **9Q-CDG** Transair Cargo rr 05.98; sJNB 6.06.98 testflight; **9G-CDG** TAC Air Svcs rr s14.06.98; sAthens opf Air Afrique/s18.12.98 opf MK AL as 9G-CDG, sATH 15.06.00 metallic no tit, sMalta 31.07.00 Continental Cargo AL lsd opf Analinda AL; **3D-CDG** s19.06.01; sPietersburg 19.06.01 bare metal, id not conf, s2004 in service from dusty African runway; **9Q-CJC** Transair Cargo by 2005?; repo as such wfu FIH 29.08.05 awaits D-check, repo being dismantled by 08.06.

N803SW   Seaboard World   Brussels

TR-LQR   Affretair   Paris CDG

A40-PA   CargoMan   Amsterdam

VP-WMJ of Affretair on dusty African runway

Source Unknown

Z-WMJ / Affretair / The National Cargo Airline of Zimbabwe, named "Captain Jack Mallock"

45816/236   N804SW
55CF Jet Trader   mfd 26.08.1965

N804SW Flying Tiger Line del 29.09.65; Slick AW NTU; Seaboard World AL lsd 29.09.65; Flying Tiger ret 22.12.68; VIASA lsd 22.12.68; Transcarga slsd 01.01.69; **YV-C-VIM** Transcarga rr 20.10.72; **N804SW** Seaboard World AL 25.07.75; EFS Bahamas lsd 01.09.76, last EFS svc OST-LOS 04.11.76; Seaboard ret 10.11.76; IAS Cargo AL lsd 10.11.76 when del LUX-LGW; **G-BIAS** IAS Cargo AL bt 08.02.78; British Air Cargo mgd 15.08.79; std Stansted, Essex; Seaboard World AL 08.80; Flying Tiger Line mgd 09.80; **N804SW** Flying Tiger Line rr 30.01.81; Challenge Air Transport lsd 08.81; Capitol AW 04.11.83; MPA Pacific Cargo lsd 12.83; own JN Associates 24.01.84; Northern Peninsula Fisheries 06.84; Barclays Bank reposs 12.86; Connie Kalitta 02.02.87; **N801CK** Connie Kalitta rr 03.88; Kal-American Int AW nn 01.03.91; Kitty Hawk Int nn 03.02.99; s str Oscoda MI 20.08.00, Kitty Hawk to Nat AcS 12.00 to be brup Oscoda, s06.01 derelict, presum brup since, canc 27.02.13.

N804SW   Berlin-Tegel   seen on 10.07.66   *Photo Ralf Manteufel*

YV-C-VIM / Transcarga, basic VIASA livery

N804SW- leased to EFS / 1976 / Ostend Photo Jacques Barbé

N804SW / EFS Bahamas, basic Seaboard cheatline / Ostend September 1976   Photo Jacques Barbé

N801CK / American International Airways / Miami 1991   via E.J. Gual

45817/248   N805SW
55CF Jet Trader   mfd 14.12.1965

N805SW Flying Tiger Line del 12.01.66; Slick AW NTU; Seaboard World AL lsd 12.01.66; Flying Tiger ret 05.03.69; **N805U** Universal AL lsd 05.04.69; Scandinavian Airlines System slsd 10.06.70 in Universal c/s; Flying Tiger ret 09.12.70; **HB-IDU** Balair 02.04.71, last svc AGP-ZRH 01.10.79; **N9110V** ONA 04.10.79; Libyan Arab AL lsd 04.10.79 and ferried ZRH-Benghazi 04.10.79; ONA ret 11.79; Aeral lsd 29.11.79; Saudia slsd 09.06.80 when del FCO-JED; Aeral ret 24.06.80, del JED-FCO 24.06.80; last Aeral service JFK-MXP 31.08.80; ONA ret 18.09.80; Libyan Arab AL lsd 23.09.80; ONA ret 13.10.80, lsd again 24.10.80, ONA ret 14.11.80; **N911R** Elan Air lsd 11.07.81; ONA ret 05.03.82; Rich Int'l AW lsd 07.01.83; ONA ret 23.08.83; National AL nn 01.12.83; Air Transport Int'l lsd 02.84; National AL ret 15.10.84; **TF-AED** AirXport 15.04.86; Eagle Air 15.08.86; **HP-1088** Aéreos Trans de Panama lsd 15.08.86; own EAS Cargo; **5N-ATS** EAS Cargo ret 02.01.87; **N808CK** Connie Kalitta 01.08.88; Kal-American Int AW nn 01.03.91; Trans Continental lsd 09.08.94; s ATL 14.12.95 no tit, Kal col, opf TCA?, sMIA 28.03.96 TC fc; **N182SK** Trans Continental rr 09.96; then old reg, rr s17.01.97, pkd Detroit YIP s22.08.99, Scott B King Trustee, own by 02.03.00, r24.05.00 TCA Creditor Trust, s str Detroit YIP 02.03.00 TCA col, GAT 19.09.00, s13.01.01, eng being removed, 25.02.01 being brup.

N805U   Universal Airlines

HB-IDU / Balair

N182SK Trans Continental / Miami 1991

via E.J. Gual

46003/401 N783FT
63AF mfd 09.1968

N783FT Flying Tiger Line del 22.10.68 in "Jumbo Jet" scheme; Air India lsd 25.11.82; Flying Tiger Line ret 07.04.83; own Cammacorp 08.83; Cammacorp ret 08.84; cvtd to DC8-73AF 10.84; **D-ADUA** German Cargo 16.10.84; own DeuL 09.88; Lufthansa Cargo nn 01.05.93; sFRA 12.07.96 xLH col, frd Macon 03.08.96 ; **N603AL** Emery WW lsd 12.09.96; AFG r8.96, WTC 21.12.99, AL ceased 13.08.01; ATI-Air Transport Int 26.09.02; own WTC, sPHX 29.05.03 new ATI col plus small BAX Global titles on top of tail, AFG to DC-8 Aircraft Two LLC 18.12.06, Cargo Aircraft Management r14.01.10 presum still lsd to ATI, s str Marana 27.03.11, sis Ottawa-GUA 28.07.11, frd CVG-MHV 04.04.12 for str, for sale 05.12 via myairlease.com, s05.13 MHV, s04.04.14, Cargo AC M. sold 25.02.14 to Flight Star Trading LLC (Ft Lauderdale FL), r02.05.14.

N783FT \ Flying Tiger Line \ Brussels

N783FT / Flying Tigers / Atlanta 1984 after -73AF conversion — via E.J. Gual

N603AL / Air Transport International, with BAX (Burlington Air Express) Global on tail — via E.J. Gual

46004/403 N784FT
63AF mfd **17.09.1968**

N784FT Flying Tiger Line del 25.10.68 in "Jumbo Jet" scheme; cvtd to DC-8-73AF 10.82; United Parcel Svc-UPS 29.12.82; **N804UP** United Parcel Svc-UPS rr 07.83; sROW 04.02.04, s15.11.07, AerSale Inc 18.06.10, canc 07.07.10 pwfu ROW

N784FT Flying Tiger Line Atlanta

N784FT Flying Tigers

N784FT United Parcel Service via E.J. Gual

46005/412   mfd 18.10.1968
63AF   f/f 09.11.1968
N785FT

N785FT Flying Tiger Line del 25.11.68; crashed into sea on appr 27.07.70 off Okinawa, Ryukyu Isl; 4 fatalities; TT 6.047h.

Accident description

The aircraft departed Los Angeles for a flight to Da Nang AFB, Vietnam with intermediate stops at San Francisco, CA, Seattle, WA, Cold Bay, AK, Tokyo, Okinawa and Cam Ranh Bay. Flight 45 departed Tokyo 09:29 for the IFR flight to Okinawa. The flight proceeded without difficulty to Okinawa, and was cleared for an en route descent to an altitude of 1,000 feet msl to make a precision radar approach to runway 18 at Naha AFB. At 11:31 the flight was advised "... have reduced visibility on final ... tower just advised approach lights and strobe lights are on ....". At 11:32:46, a new altimeter setting of 25.84 inches was given to the crew and acknowledged. The landing checklist, including full flaps, setting of radio altimeters, gear down and locked, and spoilers armed, was completed at 11:33:49. At slightly less than 5 miles from touchdown, the crew was instructed to begin the descent onto glide path and was cleared to land. The approach continued, with various heading changes and, at 11:34:53, the crew was advised that they were slightly below the glide path 3 miles from touchdown. Additional vectors were provided and at 11:35:14, 2 miles from touchdown, the crew was again advised "...dropping slightly below glide path ... you have a 10 knot tailwind." At 11:35:34, the controller advised the crew that they were on glide path. The DC-8 continued to descend and broke out of heavy rain and low clouds at an estimated altitude of 75 to 100 feet. The aircraft struck the water approximately 2,200 feet short of the runway at a speed of 144kts.

PROBABLE CAUSE: "An un-arrested rate of descent due to inattention of the crew to instrument altitude references while the pilot was attempting to establish outside visual contact in meteorological conditions which precluded such contact during that segment of a precision radar approach inbound from the Decision Height."

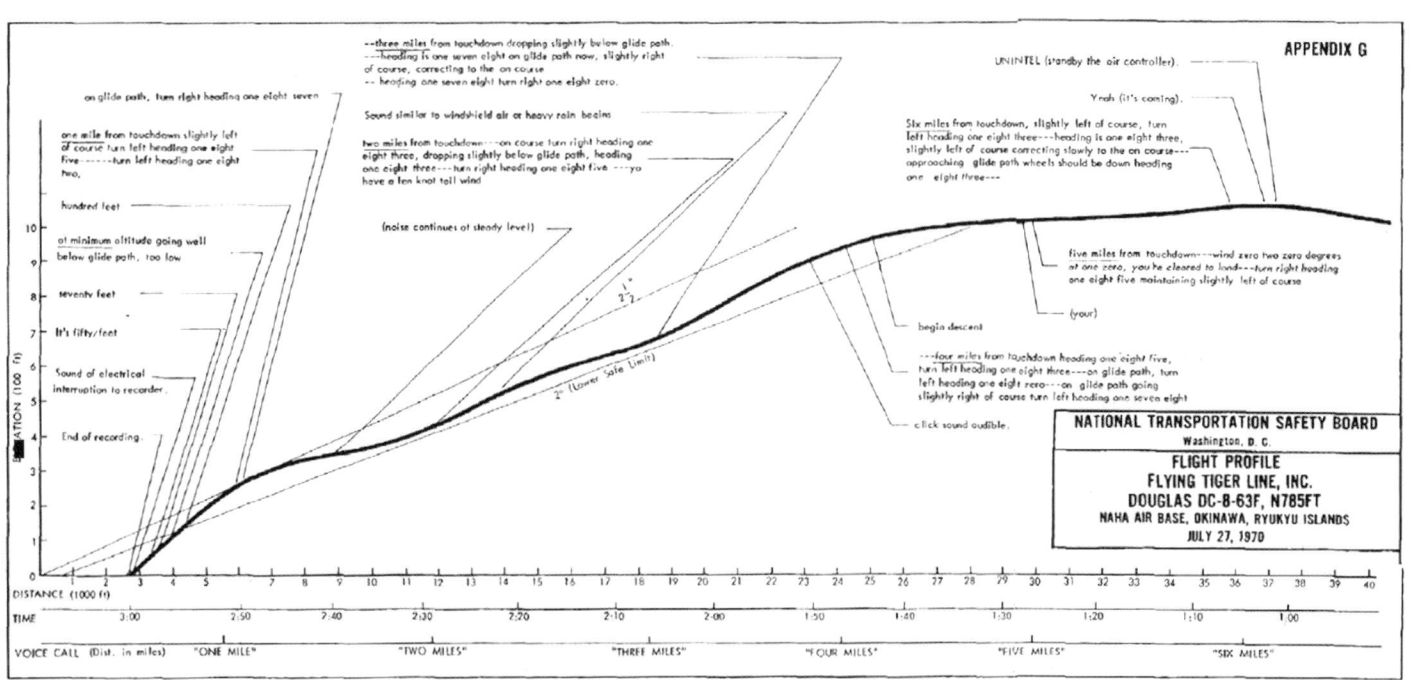

Illustration from the official accident investigation report of the National Transport Safety Bureau (NTSB)

46006/413   N786FT
63AF   mfd 23.10.1968

N786FT Flying Tiger Line del 03.12.68; cvtd to DC-8-73AF 12.82; United Parcel Svc-UPS 29.12.82; **N806UP** United Parcel Svc-UPS rr 08.83; "still" str sROW 26.10.05, presum ret in svc, repo frd SDF-ROW 26.08.08, s str 23.04.09, Aersale 28.07.10, canc 12.08.10 pwfu ROW

N786FT   Flying Tigers

N786FT   Flying Tigers   via E.J. Gual

N806UP / United Parcel Service

N806UP / seen stored at Roswell International Air Center on 19.01.06

Photo Radek Oneksiak

 **46007/422** N787FT **N787FT** Flying Tiger Line del 03.01.69; cvtd to DC-8-73AF
63AF mfd **25.11.1968** 12.82; United Parcel Svc-UPS 29.12.82; **N807UP** United
Parcel Svc-UPS rr 01.84; type wfu by 12.05.09, sROW
25.08.09, UPS to Aersale Inc 31.08.10, canc 13.09.10
pwfu

N787FT Flying Tiger Line Tokyo Haneda

N787FT Flying Tigers Ostend

46008/423   N788FT   **N788FT** Flying Tiger Line del 06.01.69; cvtd to DC-8-73AF
63AF   mfd 27.11.1968   02.83; United Parcel Svc-UPS 06.83; **N808UP** United
Parcel Svc-UPS rr 09.83; type wfu by 12.05.09, sROW
13.11.09, UPS to Aersale Inc 31.08.10, canc 13.09.10
pwfu, sROW 07.10.11 wfu

N788FT   Flying Tigers

N808UP   United Parcel Service   via E.J. Gual

46044/432　　N790FT　　**N790FT** Flying Tiger Line del 28.02.69; Air India lsd
63AF　　mfd 01.1969　　05.12.82; own Cammacorp 08.83; Cammacorp ret 10.83;

N790FT ▰ *Flying Tiger Line* ▰ *Paris Le Bourget*

N790FT ▰ *Flying Tigers*

Flying Tiger Line lsd 10.83; Cammacorp ret 07.84; cvtd 08.84; **D-ADUE** German Cargo lsd 06.08.84; own DeuL 09.88; Lufthansa Cargo nn 01.05.93; rAFG 9.96 (N?), sis 22.02.97 only DC-8-70 in full Lufthansa Cargo col, ret AFG 20.05.97; **N606AL** Emery WW lsd 24.06.97; s Dayton 19.07.97 fc, AFG to WTC 21.12.99 still Emery, AL ceased 13.08.01; BAX Global/ATI-Air Transport International s04.05.02; sMIA full ATI-BAX nc, i.s. 6.07.02, s Stansted 09.02.03, WTC to Aerolease FG 23.10.06, opb ATI, AFG to DC-8 Aircraft Two LLC 19.12.06, Cargo Aircraft Management r13.01.10 still lsd to ATI, sis BUD 13.10.11, for sale 05.12 via myairlease.com, frd BUF to Mojave 21.12.12 for str, frd MHV-Wilmington ILN 05.06.14, N-reg canc 06.10.14; **5Y-RCA** Ribway Cargo AL, due, slLN 07.10.14 ex ATI bcs, Ribway Cargo AL billboard titles, dual N/5Y-reg s29.10.14, still there 12.14

D-ADUE // Flying Tigers prior to delivery to German Cargo // 1984 // Paris Le Bourget

D-ADUE // Lufthansa Cargo // Frankfurt am Main

N606AL // ATI   via E.J. Gual

45989/371 N779FT
63AF mfd 21.05.1968

N779FT Flying Tiger Line del 28.06.68; Flying Tiger "Jumbo Jet" title on delivery; **LX-ACV** Cargolux 19.06.76; Air India lsd 09.79; Air India Cargo titles, sis Paris-Orly 24.05.80; Cargolux ret 03.80; Aero Uruguay lsd 30.04.81; Cargolux ret 12.06.82; Aer Turas lsd 01.10.82; **EI-BNA** Air Turas rr 15.04.83; Aer Turas bt 02.07.84; Saudia lsd 16.09.90; Aer Turas ret s11.96; ret then,is/s5.98 basic old Saudia col no tit, opf DHL, later repo lsd to Saudia 18.09.89-31.01.98, pkd Dublin 12.98, frd Dub-Marana 27-30.11.99 for str, basic old Saudia col, s27.01.03 id, canc 23.12.03 presum to be brup at Marana, s11.02.04 wfu basic col, s20.10.07

N779FT — Flying Tiger Line "Jumbo Jet" livery — via John Wegg

N790FT / Flying Tiger Line / Hong Kong

LX-ACV / Aero Uruguay

LX-ACV / Air India Cargo

EI-BNA / Aer Turas / Ostend　　　Photo Pol van Damme

EI-BNA / Saudia Air Cargo　　　via E.J. Gual

45990/375　　N780FT
63CF　　mfd 06.1968

N780FT Flying Tiger Line del 17.07.68 in "Jumbo Jet" scheme; **TF-CCV** Cargolux 30.06.77; Air India lsd 04.83; Cargolux ret 11.83; Evergreen Int'l AL lsd 01.84; Evergreen bt 07.84; **N816EV** Evergreen Int'l AL rr 05.01.85; cvtd to DC8-73CF 01.85, hit a mast 21.04.85 during low pass Billund, flew onwards to Berlin; Air India lsd 07.85; Air India Cargo titles + Evergreen cheatlines painted both in red; Evergreen ret 04.86, lsd again 01.88, ret 11.88; TNT Express lsd 01.07.92; s white, TNT logo JFK 7.92; ret 03.94 ; United Parcel Svc-UPS S lsd 08.04.94; due ret 4.96? sis 15.06.94 white, EvSPC r8.94 ; **N816UP** DHL AW r3.95; UPS lsd 27.03.95 ret to DHL 12.04.96; **N807DH** DHL AW rr 06.96; s22.07.96 full DHL ; Astar Air Cargo nn 30.06.03; sis BRU 21.04.10 DHL yellow fc, Astar USA LLC r13.01.11, frd CVG-IGM 02.06.12 for str, s21.11.12, Aerotradex Inc (Hollywood FL) 30.01.13, r31.01.13, frd IGM-VCV 03.02.13, s03.13 white/dark blue cs, no reg, Aerotradex to Transpacific Heavylift Inc 29.03.13; SkyBus Jet Cargo Inc 29.03.13; r09.04.13 due for cargo ops from Las Vegas, frd Victorville-Port Moresby 17-18.08.13 wlsd to Heavylift Cargo AL, canc 27.08.13 to Peru; **OB-2059-P** Transpacific Heavylift 27.08.13; repo first svc 20.12.13 to operated to BNE, POM and more, operator aka Peruvian AL, then repo fis 11.03.14 BNE-Nauru, frd BNE–Lima 11-12.06.14 for maintenance, ret LIM-PPG-BNE 22-23.06.14, sis BNE 09.07.14, ret to Peruvian AL, frd BNE-KUL 05.10.14, arr Ostend 16.10.14, based for Ebola relief flights but no flights by 12.14.

N780FT　Flying Tiger Line　"Jumbo Jet" titles are still visible

N780FT / Flying Tigers / Amsterdam

N816EV / Evergreen International

N816EV / TNT Express Worldwide / Pinal Airpark (Marana)   via E.J. Gual

N807DH / DHL / Miami   via E.J. Gual

OB-2059-P / Ostend February 2015   Photo Michel Huart

45991/380   N781FT
63CF   mfd 07.1968

N781FT Flying Tiger Line del 26.07.68 in "Jumbo Jet" scheme; own Cammacorp 08.83; cvtd to DC8-73CF 06.84; **D-ADUI** German Cargo 10.07.84; own DeL 09.88; Lufthansa Cargo nn 01.05.93; **N602AL** AFG r06.96; frd FRA-Naples 12.06.96 basic LH col ; Emery World AL lsd 09.09.96; sBRU white 10.96/s28.03.97 San Diego,10.97 Madrid white, sDayton OH 25.03.98, AFG to WTC 21.12.99, still Emery, AL ceased 13.08.01, frd Roswell-San Jose (CR) 13.06.02 after str; ATI-Air Transport Int lsd 23.12.02; WTC, to Aerolease FG 23.10.06, opb ATI, AFG to DC-8 Aircraft Two LLC 20.12.06, Cargo Aircraft Management r13.01.10 still lsd to ATI, sis BFI 13.05.10, dam Toledo 22.02.11 slid off taxiway into a snowbank, sis 10.11, for sale 05.12 via myairlease.com, s str Mojave 19.05.12; Bravo Int AW/Stabo Air 29.12.13; frd MHV-IAH-OST 29-30.12.13 basic ATI cs, depa OST 01.01.14, N-reg canc 29.05.14; **TT-DBC** Bravo Int AW rr, s27.01.15, sNBO ex ATI cs no titles, based at Fujairah

N781FT   Flying Tiger Jumbo Jet in Long Beach, 1968

N781FT / Flying Tiger Line / San Francisco

N781FT / Flying Tigers / Frankfurt am Main

Coll. Guy Van Herbruggen

D-ADUI - Flying Tigers ◣ in 1984, in front of UTA Industries hangars ◣ Paris Le Bourget

N602AL ◣ Emery Worldwide

N-602AL ◣ in 1997 on a DHL flight ◣ Brussels

Photo: Michel Huart

TT-DBC ◣ Bravo Int'l Airways, still in basic ATI livery
◣ Nairobi January 2015   Photo: Michel Huart

46002/394 N782FT
63CF mfd 15.08.1968

N782FT Flying Tiger Line del 17.09.68 in "Jumbo Jet" scheme; **LX-BCV** Cargolux 07.10.75; TF-BCV Cargolux rr 27.11.75; **LX-TAM** Transportación Aérea Mexicana NTU; **LX-BCV** Trans. Aérea Mexicana lsd 31.03.84; Cargolux ret 01.07.84; **N815EV** Evergreen Int'l 15.07.84; cvtd 02.85; lsd to TNT 3.05.92/tfd to Ev SPC 29.04.94 ; **N815UP** United Parcel Svc-UPS lsd 29.04.94; s24.06.94 in white, DHL r3.95 ; **N806DH** DHL AW ret 12.04.96; sDetW 25.04.95 white/rr 6.96, DHL fc 6.08.96, aborted take off 25.09.01 went off runway Mexico City, presum repairable; Astar Air Cargo nn 30.06.03; Astar USA LLC r13.01.11, frd CVG-IGM 27.05.12 for str, s21.11.12, s wfu 24.10.13

N782FT — Flying Tiger Line

LX-BCV — TAM Mexico

N806DH — DHL — Miami December 1996   via E.J. Gual

46045/441   N791FT
63CF   mfd 05.02.1969

N791FT Flying Tiger Line del 17.03.69; American Flyers AL lsd 01.05.69; Flying Tiger ret 30.04.70; SATA lsd 07.75; Flying Tiger ret 11.75; El Al lsd 22.03.79; Flying Tiger ret 30.04.79; National Funding Corp 03.84; cvtd 03.84; N791FT Emery WW lsd 06.04.84; own BAT 01.90; Air India Cargo slsd s23.08.94; sToronto; Emery WW ret 08.95; GECC own 29.09.95, FSB 11.04.01 still Emery WW, AL ceased 13.08.01, Polaris LI to Aeroturbine 31.10.02, s str Roswell 28.12.02, s09.07.03, repo scrapped by 06.02.04, Aeroturbine r18.11.04 so presum still str somewhere? canc 17.05.06 ROW brup

N791FT   American Flyers Airline

N791FT   leased to SATA in 1975   Rotterdam

N791FT ▰ Brussels 10 April 1976   Photo Jacques Barbé

N791FT ▰ Emery ▰ Atlanta 1984

N791FT ▰ Emery Worldwide livery, no titles

N791FT ▰ Emery Worldwide

46046/444   N792FT
63CF   mfd 02.1969

N792FT Flying Tiger Line del 21.03.69; American Flyers AL lsd 26.05.69; Flying Tiger Line ret 21.05.70; cvtd to DC-8-73CF 01.84; Emery WW 26.01.84; sOstend 11.91 DHL tit, SSB&TC r5.10.99 opb Emery, s hangar Smyrna 6.08.01 str?, AL ceased 13.08.01, SSB&TC to LOGAIR LLC 30.08.02, WTC 25.11.02, sRoswell 02.02.03 Emery WW fc, s09.07.03, s04.02.04, frd SPIM-TUS-Sacramento KMCC 29-30.03.05; **N604BX** ATI-Air Transport Int'l 29.03.05; bt ex WTC, rr res 10.05.05, rr 08.06.05, frd GYR-Toluca 29.07.05 fc, ATI to DC-8 Aircraft Two LLC 22.08.07, Cargo Aircraft Management r13.01.10 still lsd to ATI, sis BUD 03.03.10, SJC 12.09.11, for sale 05.12 via myairlease.com, not wfu yet, sis 24.05.12 CGN/OST, frd to PHL-MHV 22-23.12.12, canc 01.05.14 wfu MHV

N792FT — American Flyers Airline

N792FT — Flying Tiger Line

N792FT / Flying Tigers

N792FT / Emery Worldwide / Atlanta / via E.J.Gual

N792FT / Emery Worldwide operating DHL flight / Brussels / via E.J.Gual

46047/447   N793FT
63CF   mfd 26.02.1969

N793FT Flying Tiger Line del 31.03.69; ONA lsd 04.04.69; Flying Tiger ret 30.09.70; Trans International AL lsd 01.06.78; Flying Tiger Line ret 27.09.78; own Cammacorp 08.83; Cammacorp ret 08.84; cvtd 09.84; **D-ADUO** German Cargo lsd 10.09.84; own DeuL 09.88; Lufthansa Cargo nn 01.05.93; AFG r9.96 (N?), ret 4.97 ; **N604AL** Emery WW lsd 20.04.97; rgd 4.97 AFG, s4.10.97 BRU full Emery WW col,opf DHL, AFG to WTC 21.12.99, AL ceased 13.08.01, s str Roswell 28.12.02 fc, frd to Lima 15.04.03, for?; N809DH Astar Air Cargo r13.04.04; reg res 27.02.04 WTC, sis SEA 16.04.04 in svc, sis 03.05 nc, sMiami 02.09.06 white, s24.09.06 as **PP-BEL** white, frd to Lima (24.09.06?) for maint, canc 26.10.06; PP-BEL BETA Cargo (Brazilian Express Transportes Aéreos) 26.10.06; sManaus 04.10.09 engines 2 and 4 missing; pwfu, s05.10, s12.10 Sao Paulo GRU complete, s05.11 str, s10.14 wfu

N793FT   Overseas National

N793FT   Trans International Cargo, Flying Tigers cheatline

N793FT   Flying Tigers

D-ADUO / Flying Tigers, before delivery to German Cargo / August 1984 / Dallas Fort Worth

N604AL / Emery Worldwide

46086/478 N794FT
63CF mfd 11.07.1969

N794FT Flying Tiger Line del 04.08.69; manuf 11.07.69; World AW lsd 06.11.75, seen LGW 16.11.75 in full WO c/s; Flying Tiger ret 09.05.76; Trans International AL lsd 01.03.78; **N870TV** Trans International AL rr 04.78; Transamerica AL nn 01.10.79; Flying Tiger Line ret 12.06.84; own Bendix Corp 12.06.84; cvtd to DC8-73CF 07.84; Bendix Corp ret 19.07.84; Emery WW lsd 19.07.84; (opf DHL JP92),RFC r12.94, str s10.12.01 Kingman basic col no tit, TFC N870TV/7 Inc, to WFBN 16.04.02, s str 19.05.02, s20.08.02, s26.01.03 Emery WW col, WFBN to AeroTurbine 11.04.03, s24.12.03 basic Emery WW col, s26.04.04 no engines, s30.01.05 in scrapping area, s08.09.05, still IGM 28.02.06 Emery WW col, WFBN 24.04.06, r31.05.06 pwfu IGM (not cancelled yet), s16.10.06 missing many parts, s08.05.07 engines are being mounted, prepared for svc, frd Kingman-GYR 24.03.07 not to South America… s str Goodyear 20.11.07; **PP-BEM** BETA Cargo 23.01.08; frd GYR-Miami-Lima, due for svc, N-reg canc 06.08.08, sis GRU 26.09.08, POA 02.06.10, repo str Manaus by 05.11, AL lost licence 07.12

N794FT Flying Tigers

N794FT / World Airways / Paris Orly

N794FT / World Airways / Paris Orly

N870TV / Trans International Cargo

N870TV / Brussels / Coll. Guy Van Herbruggen

N870TV Emery / Amsterdam

46103/483 N795FT
63CF mfd 21.07.1969

N795FT Flying Tiger Line del 29.08.69, i/s 02.09.69; Bendix Corp 13.06.84; cvtd 06.84; Emery WW lsd 13.06.84; RFC r12.94, sToronto 7.07.00, Smyrna TN 12.08.00 fc (str?), AL ceased 13.08.01, frd Dayton-Kingman 15.11.01 for str, s19.05.02, s20.08.02, s26.01.03 Emery WW col, s18.05.03, s20.08.03 basic col, AeroTurbine 31.10.03, s24.12.03 no engines, s26.04.04, s30.01.05 in scrapping area; **PP-BET** BETA Cargo 05.10.05; frd Kingman-Miami 13.05.05, to Lima 14.05.05 ex Emery col, for overhaul and then to Brazil ar 07.05, op. not confirmed, canc 05.10.05 to Brazil, s12.11.05 GRU fc, r17.11.05, s str MAO 05.10, s07.12 molded, at least one engine missing, at least two engines still there, s10.08.14 poor condition

N795FT Flying Tiger Line

N795FT Flying Tigers

N795FT / Emery *via E.J. Gual*

N795FT / Emery, stored at Kingman, AZ

46104/488 mfd 26.08.1969 **N796FT** Flying Tiger Line del 03.10.69, i/s 07.10.69; Air India lsd 16.08.81; Air India Cargo titles + basic Flying Tiger
63CF N796FT

N796FT Flying Tiger Line

N796FT Flying Tigers

c/s, sis 22.08.82 Frankfurt; Flying Tiger Line ret 25.11.82; Connecticut NB 05.84; Emery WW lsd 05.84; cvtd 05.84, SSB&TC r31.05.00, frd Dothan-Marana 4.01.01, LOGAIR LLC 30.08.02, WTC 25.11.02, s str Roswell 02.02.03 Emery WW col, s09.07.03, s04.02.04, frd to Miami 29.06.04 full Emery col, frd to Lima 03.07.04, Aerofreighter LLC/WTC reg canc 27.10.04; **PP-BEX** BETA Cargo 30.10.04; arr Sao Paulo fc, sLima 12.11 wfu

N796FT / Air India Cargo

N796FT / Emery & Purolator

PP-BEX / BETA (Brazilian Express Transportes Aereos) / Sao Paulo

via E.J. Gual

/ **46138** N797FT
63CF mfd -
N797FT Flying Tiger Line; ORDER CANCELLED, NOT BUILT

DC-8s EITHER BOUGHT OR LEASED ON THE USED AIRCRAFT MARKET

45858/274   N789FT
55CF Jet Trader   **mfd 21.07.1966**

N1509U Douglas; Panagra lsd 02.09.66; Braniff mgd 01.02.67; Solid Pastel Orange c/s; Seaboard World AL slsd 05.05.67; Braniff ret 07.08.67, Douglas ret 11.67; **CF-CPT** Canadian Pacific AL 17.11.67; CP Air nn 04.69; **C-FCPT** CP Air rr 01.01.74; **N789FT** Flying Tiger Line lsd 26.09.77, seen LAX 09.10.77 ex FT c/s; **C-FCPT** CP Air ret 01.02.78; **G-BSKY** IAS Cargo AL 15.02.78; lsd Alitalia 06.08.78, ret 03.09.78; British Cargo AL mgd 15.08.79; std Bournemouth 03.80; C Itoh & Co 28.07.80; **HC-BJT** Andes AL 17.02.82; **3D-ADV** African Int'l AW 02.08.85; **5N-ATY** Flash AL 20.04.87; wfu s6.91 Ostend, 1 eng,& parts missing, s9.91 some engines, horiz stabilizer...missing; **EL-AJQ** Liberia World AL 08.09.93; sis 14.08.97, sOstend white 16.08.97, s5.99, ATH 8.08.99 white, sGVA 9.06.00 black/red ACR tail logo, white fus (not 45686, EL-AJQ nr 1), s10.00 all white, repo dam 12.10.00, last flight in Europe 01.01 departing to Uganda, this AC also (see EL-AJO) has been involved in illegal transports; **3C-QRG** Air Cargo Plus s16.11.01; sis Nairobi 16.11.01 small CP Avtn titles on fus, ex reg EL-AJQ still vis, sSHJ 17.01.02 white col, small CP Avtn titl, id 21.05.02 now grey tail, sSHJ 5.08.02 white no titles; Spirit of Africa AL/Blue Nile s04.12.02; sSHJ white fus. blue tail, due; **9Q-CAN** Kinshasa AW s09.01.03; sSHJ, sKinshasa 11.09.03, s21.02.04, str, bt by Hewa Bora AW for parts 09.07 for cn 45764, s wfu Kinshasa 12.05.09

N1509U — *Braniff International*

CF-CPT — *CP Air*

9Q-CAN — *Kinshasa* — *parked at Sharjah*

◢45938/331 N860FT
61CF mfd 05.12.1967

N8960T Trans International AL 02.02.69; **N804U** Universal AL lsd 29.01.71; **N8960T** Trans International AL ret 05.05.72; Seaboard World AL lsd 30.04.73; Loftleidir slsd 06.05.73; Seaboard World AL ret 22.10.74; Air Cargo Egypt slsd 01.04.77; Pakistan Int'l slsd 15.07.77; Air Cargo Egypt ret 12.77; Seaboard World AL ret 26.03.78; Trans International AL ret 26.03.78; **N860FT** Flying Tiger Line lsd 03.04.78; Transamerica AL ret 18.07.84; United Parcel Svc-UPS 16.05.85; cvtd to DC8-71CF 07.85; **N701UP** United Parcel Svc-UPS rr 10.85; frd SDF-ROW 26.08.08 str, s01.02.10, UPS to AerSale 26.02.10, canc 01.04.10 pwfu ROW, sROW 07.10.11 wfu

N804U / Universal Airlines / London Gatwick

N8960T / Trans International

N8960T / Loftleidir Icelandic

N8960T Seaboard World Zürich Kloten

N8960T Air Cargo Egypt 1977

N8960T Pakistan International Cargo Paris Orly 1977

N860FT / Flying Tigers — via E.J.Gual

N701UP / United Parcel Service — via E.J.Gual

45900/316 N861FT
61CF mfd 09.1967

N8962T Trans International AL 30.11.67; **N803U** Universal AL lsd 26.03.70; **N8962T** Trans International AL ret 05.05.72; Seaboard World AL lsd 24.05.73; Loftleidir Icelandic slsd 30.05.73; Seaboard ret 08.10.73; Cargolux slsd 08.10.73; **TF-BCV** Cargolux rr 10.73; **N8962T** Seaboard World AL ret 06.05.74; Loftleidir Icelandic slsd 06.05.74 named "Eirikur randi"; Seaboard ret 10.04.75; Trans International AL ret 31.05.76; **N861FT** Flying Tiger Line lsd 01.06.78; Transamerica AL ret 06.05.84; Trans International AL lsd 09.84; United Parcel Svc-UPS 16.05.85; **N700UP** United Parcel Svc-UPS rr 08.85; cvtd to DC8-71CF 09.85, type wfu by 12.05.09, frd PHL-ROW 19.05.09 for str, AerSale Inc 28.05.10, r17.06.10, sROW 07.10.11 wfu, s04.13, canc 15.09.14

N8962T Trans International

N8962T Loftleidir Icelandic, named "Eirikur randi"
London Heathrow

N8962T Seaboard World Rotterdam

Photo D. Booster

N861FT / Flying Tigers — via E.J. Gual

N861FT / Flying Tigers

N861FT — Flying Tigers — stored Las Vegas in 1982 via E.J.Gual

N861FT — Trans International via E.J.Gual

N700UP — United Parcel Service via E.J.Gual

45948/321 N862FT
61CF mfd 20.10.1967

N8955U Saturn AW 28.12.67; Seaboard World AW lsd 20.01.75; EFS Bahamas slsd 01.09.76; Seaboard ret 01.04.77; Trans International AL ret 25.04.77; Capitol Int'l AW lsd 26.10.77; TAI ret 24.01.78; **N862FT** Flying Tiger Line lsd 01.02.78; Emery WW slsd 20.08.82; Flying Tiger Line ret 26.04.84; Transamerica AL ret 30.12.84; United Parcel Svc-UPS 16.05.85; cvtd to DC8-71CF 08.85; **N748UP** United Parcel Svc-UPS rr 09.85; W/O 08.02.06 Philadelphia PA 0(3) on board fire in aft cargo area, burnt through fuselage after emergency landing (AC in new colors).

Accident description

UPS flight 1307, a regular night-time package flight from Atlanta (ATL) to Philadelphia (PHL), departed Atlanta at 22:42 EST. Just after receiving clearance to land at runway 27R, the DC-8 crew reported that they had a smoke warning light come on: "Cleared to land, and ah listen we just got a cargo smoke indicator come on can we have the equipment?". The Tower controller replied: "Okay, I'll do that ..the cargo smoke indicator....ah... souls on board and amount of fuel Sir?" UPS1307 reported three souls on board and two hours worth of fuel. About a minute later the controller cleared the fight to land at runway 27L, which is 1006 feet (308 m) longer than runway 27R. The crew confirms the clearance, but continues their approach to 27R. The tower controller notices this and queries: "..1307 Heavy just confirming that your are lined up to the left side and it appears you are lined up to the right." UPS1307 replies: "I am sorry I thought we were cleared for the right..uh.. are we cleared to land on the right?" The tower controller then clears them to land on 27R and informs the fire department about this. Smoke was coming from the aircraft as it landed. The crew evacuated and the fire services started fighting the fire. The blaze was reported under control by about 04:00.

PROBABLE CAUSE: "The National Transportation Safety Board determines that the probable cause of this accident was an in-flight cargo fire that initiated from an unknown source, which was most likely located within cargo container 12, 13, or 14. Contributing to the loss of the aircraft were inadequate certification test requirements for smoke and fire detection systems and the lack of an on-board fire suppression system. "

Wreck still there ar 07.06, to Aeroturbine 06.09.06, canc 06.10.06.

N8955U / Saturn

N8955U — Trans International

N862FT — Flying Tigers

N748UP / United Parcel Service

N748UP / PHL 08.02.06   Photos NTSB

45949/329
61CF
N863FT
mfd 27.11.1967

N8956U Saturn AW 30.01.68; Seaboard World AW lsd 27.11.74; EFS Cargo slsd 06.75; Seaboard ret 02.76; National AW slsd 22.04.76; Seaboard ret 18.10.76; EFS Bahamas slsd 04.11.76; Seaboard ret 01.04.77; **HS-TGF** Thai AW lsd 06.06.77; **N8956U** Trans International AL ret 31.03.79; **N863FT** Flying Tiger Line lsd 20.04.79; Transamerica AL ret 30.12.84; United Parcel Svc-UPS 16.05.85; **N705UP** United Parcel Svc-UPS rr 09.85; cvtd to DC8-71CF 10.85, type wfu by 12.05.09, s str ROW 23.09.09, UPS to AerSale 26.02.10, canc 30.03.10 pwfu ROW

N8956U Saturn

HS-TGF Thai International

N863FT / Flying Tigers / Los Angeles / June 1979 Photo John Wegg

N705UP / United Parcel Service

93

45952/338   N864FT
61CF   mfd 01.1968

N8788R Trans Caribbean AW 29.02.68 named "Bennet C"; Trans International AL lsd 26.04.71; American AL ret 01.05.72; Saturn AW 01.05.72; Seaboard World AW lsd 28.02.75; EFS Bahamas slsd 01.09.76; Seaboard ret 01.04.77; **HS-TGG** Thai AW lsd 15.06.77; **N864FT** Trans International AL ret 31.03.79; Flying Tiger Line lsd 20.04.79; std Las Vegas McCarran 81; ONA slsd 10.04.81; National AL nn 01.12.83; Flying Tiger ret 30.12.84; Transamerica AL ret 30.12.84; wfu & std Marana AZ; United Parcel Svc-UPS 16.05.85; **N752UP** United Parcel Svc-UPS rr 10.85; cvtd to DC8-71CF 01.86, last UPS rev DC-8 flight 12.05.09 PHL-SDF, s str ROW 23.09.09, AerSale Inc 28.05.10, r17.06.10, sROW 07.10.11 wfu, s04.13, canc 18.09.14

N8788R Trans Caribbean

N8788R EFS Bahamas   Photo D. Booster

N8788R Seaboard World, Saturn basic livery, sub-leased to EFS Cargo

HS-TGG / Thai International

N864FT / Flying Tigers / Los Angeles / May 1982

Photo John Wegg

45939/351 N867FT
61CF mfd 05.03.1968

N801U Universal AL 18.04.68; Capitol Int'l AW lsd 18.04.68; Universal AL ret 30.09.68; **N867F** ONA 01.05.72; Capitol Int'l AW lsd 16.04.73; ONA ret 13.09.73; Seaboard World AL lsd 20.03.74; Korean AL slsd 02.04.74; Seaboard World AL ret 25.02.75; ONA ret 01.03.75; later named "Victorious"; **N867FT** Flying Tiger Line lsd 16.12.77; Flying Tiger bt 08.78; Pacific East Air lsd 01.08.82; Flying Tiger ret 09.01.84; National AL lsd 01.09.84; Flying Tiger ret 31.12.84; United Parcel Svc-UPS 30.04.85; cvtd to DC8-71CF 06.85; **N703UP** United Parcel Svc-UPS rr 10.85; type wfu by 12.05.09, UPS to AerSale 26.02.10, canc 30.03.10 pwfu ROW, s11.09.10 wfu

N867FT   Overseas National Airways

N867FT   Flying Tigers   Pinal Airpark (Marana)   via E.J. Gual

N867FT / Pacific East Air / Los Angeles — via E.J. Gual

N703UP / United Parcel Service

45950/354 N868FT
61CF mfd 15.03.1968

N802U Universal AL 26.04.68; Capitol Int'l AW lsd 26.04.68; Universal AL ret 30.09.68; **N868F** ONA 01.05.72; Seaboard World AL lsd 22.03.73; Loftleidir Icelandic slsd 25.04.73; Seaboard ret 18.09.73; Korean AL slsd 16.03.74; Seaboard ret 21.04.75; ONA ret 26.04.75 and named "Eagle"; **N868FT** Flying Tiger Line 21.12.77; United Parcel Svc-UPS 08.06.85; cvtd to DC-8-71CF 07.85; **N750UP** United Parcel Svc-UPS rr 12.85; sis 13.08.05 Louisville nc, s str ROW 15.11.07, s11.09, Aersale Inc 28.01.10, canc 19.04.10 pwfu ROW, sROW 07.10.11 wfu

N802U ◣ Capitol

N802U ◣ Universal Airlines ◣ Frankfurt am Main

N868F ◣ Seaboard World

N868FT / Flying Tigers / Miami / 30.07.83 — Coll. Guy Van Herbruggen

N750UP / San Juan 1998 — Photo Antonio R. Rivera

45961/361   N3931A
62CF-H   mfd 11.04.1968

N8964U Douglas; manuf 11.04.68; **I-DIWQ** Alitalia 30.06.68, named "Ciclope"; s 01.69 JFK Alitalia Cargo System titles; std Marana 06.81; **N3931A** Sea & Sun Avtn 04.83; still at Marana 05.83; Flying Tiger Line lsd 06.84; Sea&Sun ret 12.84, CIS Corp 01.12.85, Aerolease Int. 05.05.87, IAC Leasing Corp 05.06.87; Hawaiian AL lsd 05.06.87; own FSBoU 28.09.87, ret 02.93; wfu s30.03.93 Kingman AZ; John Hancock repo 13.10.93; own State Street Trust & Bank 15.10.93; **C-FHAA** Advance Air Charters lsd r18.10.93; ret 01.07.95; wfu sKingman 03.08.95 xAdv col no tit (Trans Am Express); **N3931A** Kal-American Int'l 15.11.95; s3.01.96 Newark,xAdvance col, sPHX 05.01.96 as **N3931**, also seen LAX 01.96 as such, probably painting mistake; **N818CK** Kal-American Int'l rr 05.96; Kitty Hawk Int'l nn 03.02.99; MIA-MHV 18.05.00, s3.07.00 str, s18.09.00 full AIA col, Kitty Hawk, reposs 23.09.02 Mellon US Leasing, C&L Avtn LLC 23.09.02; **N71CX** ATI-Air Transport Int'l 11.03.03; frd Mojave-Miami 04.04.03, ATI r06.05.03, rr 24.09.03, DC-8 Aircraft Two LLC 28.08.07, opb ATI, sis ar 03.10.08 McClellan, Cargo Aircraft Management r30.12.09 still lsd to ATI, sis 17.05.11 Patrick AFB-BWI, frd Sacramento MCC-Mojave 30.01.13 for storage, s08.05.13, Cargo A.M. sold to GRG Aircraft and Leasing 25.02.14, canc 01.05.14 wfu MHV

N3931A   August 1984   Coll. Guy Van Herbruggen

45929/367 **N624FT**
63   mfd 07.05.1968

N19B Douglas test reg; **CF-CPS** CP Air 16.06.68 named "Empress of Hong Kong"; **N624FT** Flying Tiger Line lsd 19.06.68; **CF-CPS** CP Air ret 01.07.69, named "Empress of Madrid"; **C-FCPS** CP Air rr 01.01.74 and re-named "Empress of Sydney"; std Las Vegas-McCarran; Worldways AL sold 01.03.83, i/s 19.06.83 YYZ-LGW; **N782AL** Aerolease Financial Group 28.12.90; Burl/ATI-Air Transport Int lsd 15.10.91; sMIA 03.01.94 white, own AERO,lsd 10.01.94,sMIA 20.02.94 full ATI col; W/O 16.02.95 Kansas City 3(i) cr on TO and caught fire; fuselage s wfu Dodson's scrapyard, Rantoul KS 10.04; TT 77.096h, remains s17.10.11.

N624FT   CP Air basic   Los Angeles 1968   Coll. Jacques Guillem via John Wegg

CF-CPS   Canadian Pacific "Empress of Madrid"   via E.J.Gual

C-FCPS   CP Air SkyBus/Aérobus "Empress of Sydney"   via E.J.Gual

C-FCPS   Air Algérie, Worldways basic c/s   Amsterdam

Accident description

At 20:21 LT the DC-8 prepared to take-off from RWY 01L for a flight to Westover AFB with the no. 1 engine inoperative. But the aircraft lost directional control and the crew aborted the take-off. Six minutes afterwards they attempted to take-off for the second time. At 980m into the take-off roll the DC-8 started to veer to the left. At 1160m the aircraft rotated with a tail strike but the tail remained in contact with the runway for another 250m. At 1600m the DC-8 finally became airborne and climbed to 30m before crashing into the ground, left wing-first. The wreckage came to a halt at 2300m.

PROBABLE CAUSE: "(1) The loss of directional control by the pilot in command during the takeoff roll, and his decision to continue the takeoff and initiate a rotation below the computed rotation airspeed, resulting in a premature lift-off, further loss of control and collision with the terrain. (2) The flight crew's lack of understanding of the three-engine takeoff procedures, and their decision to modify those procedures. (3) The failure of the company to ensure that the flight crew had adequate experience, training, and rest to conduct the non-routine flight. Contributing to the accident was the inadequacy of Federal Aviation Administration oversight of Air Transport International and Federal Aviation Administration flight and duty time regulations that permitted a substantially reduced flight crew rest period when conducting a nonrevenue ferry flight under 14 Code of Federal Regulations Part 91."

N782AL

Photos NTSB

45928/334 **N625FT**
63   mfd **18.12.1967**

CF-CPQ CP Air 24.02.68, named "Empress of Lima"; **N625FT** Flying Tiger Line lsd 02.07.68; **CF-CPQ** CP Air ret 30.12.68, re-named "Empress of Hong Kong"; dmgd 29.01.71 at SYD when struck by a rotating Trans-Australia Airlines 727-76 (VH-TJA) while backtracking on the active runway, repaired; **C-FCPQ** CP Air rr 01.01.74; re-named Empress of Ontario" 19.08.80; s stored Las Vegas-Mc-Carran 09.01.83; Worldways AL 01.03.83, i/s YYZ-LAS 19.05.83; **N780AL** Aerolease Financial Group 28.12.90; lst Airborne X 21.06.91; **N817AX** Airborne Express rr 11.91; Airborne bt 30.03.92; s Wilmington OH 18.08.02 pkd next to scrapping area, s10.03, s Lake Charles CWF 27.12.06 oc, minus parts to be brup, canc 15.05.07

N625FT ◤ CP Air basic ◤ Los Angeles October 1968   *Photo Jacques Guillem via John Wegg*

C-FCPQ ◤ Worldways Canada

N780AL ◤ Miami   *via E.J.Gual*

CF-CPQ / CP Air "Empress of Hong Kong" / London Gatwick

Accident description

At approximately 2137 hours Eastern Standard Time on 29 January 1971, a Trans-Australia Airlines Boeing 727 aircraft, VH-TJA, struck the tail fin of a Canadian Pacific Airlines DC8-63 aircraft, CF-CPQ, whilst the former was taking off on Runway 16 at Sydney (Kingsford-Smith) Airport, New South Wales. Both aircraft were engaged in regular public transport services and the Boeing 727 aircraft continued with its take-off but landed again at Sydney Airport 40 minutes later after dumping fuel and when preparations for the emergency landing had been completed. At the time of the collision the DC8-63 aircraft was on the ground, having just landed, and it taxied under its own power to the parking apron. Both aircraft were substantially damaged in the collision but none of the 240 persons on board the two aircraft was injured.

CF-CPQ / Illustrations from the official accident investigation report of the Australian Transport Safety Bureau

46109/493 N772FT
63CF mfd **10.09.1969**

N8642 Seaboard World AL 23.10.69; Loftleidir Icelandic lsd 04.05.75; Seaboard ret 20.09.75; lsd again 02.11.76; Seaboard World AL ret 04.01.77; ONA lsd 25.03.77; Seaboard ret 12.05.77; Air India lsd 31.12.77; Air India Cargo titles, white fuselage, sisLHR 30.03.78; Seaboard ret 01.04.79; Loftleidir Icelandic lsd 01.04.79; Icelandair mgd 79; **N772FT** Flying Tiger Line ret 30.11.80; Air India lsd 01.12.80; own ONA 08.05.81; Flying Tiger Line lsd 08.08.81; Flying Tiger bt 01.84; cvtd to DC8-73CF 01.84; United Parcel Svc-UPS 22.01.84; **N809UP** United Parcel Svc-UPS rr 06.84; s str Roswell 15.11.07, UPS sold to Aersale Inc 30.09.10, canc 18.10.10 pwfu

N8642 Seaboard World

N8642 Loftleidir Icelandic Stockholm Arlanda September 1973

N8642 / Air India Cargo

N772FT / Flying Tigers / Zürich Kloten

N772FT — Flying Tigers — Atlanta — 1984 — via E.J. Gual

N809UP — United Parcel Service — via E.J. Gual

45966/393   N773FT
63CF   mfd **12.08.1968**
N8632 Seaboard World AL 18.09.69; Saudia lsd 01.03.77 in full SV c/s; **N773FT** Saudia rr 28.11.80; Flying Tiger Line ret 30.04.81 (as SB merged with FT 09.80); Air India lsd 08.08.81; Air India Cargo titles + Flying Tiger basic c/s, sis Zurich 20.06.82; Flying Tiger Line ret 05.12.82; cvtd to DC8-73CF 04.84; United Parcel Svc-UPS 07.05.84; **N866UP** United Parcel Svc-UPS rr 08.84; s str Roswell 15.11.07, UPS to Aersale Inc 28.02.11, canc 05.04.11 wfu ROW

N8632 / Saudia Air Cargo

N773FT / small red Flying Tigers titles, basic Saudia c/s

N773FT ◣ Air India Cargo, Flying Tigers basic c/s

N773FT ◣ Flying Tigers (no titles)

N773FT / Flying Tigers

N773FT / Flying Tigers, converted as -73CF / Montréal–Dorval 1984

 **46087/454** N774FT
63CF mfd 03.1969

N864F Capitol

N864F Saudi Arabian Airlines, Capitol basic c/s

N864F ONA 28.04.69, named "Serene"; Air Afrique lsd 10.77; ONA ret 11.77; Seaboard World AL 17.12.77; Capitol Int'l AW lsd 29.05.79; Seaboard ret 27.11.79; Saudia lsd 30.11.79; **N774FT** Flying Tiger Line 03.81; ONA 21.04.81; Wien Air Alaska lsd 10.05.81; **N906R** Wien Air Alaska rr 10.81; ONA ret 09.07.82; Airlift Int'l lsd 05.11.82; ONA ret 16.07.83; Air India lsd 01.09.83; ONA ret 10.83; lsd again 11.83; National AL ret 12.84; own ATASCO Lsg 01.85; Air India slsd 02.85; National AL ret 01.07.85; Emery WW 03.86; own Aerolease Financial 13.06.88;ret AFG 01.06.95; ATI-Air Transport Int'l lsd 25.07.95; AFG to WTC 21.12.99 still ATI, s str Marana 5.02.02 ATI col; Fine Air lsd 18.10.02; own WTC, repo lsd to Arrow Air (?)/ Aerofreighter LLC (own) s "still" str Marana 27.01.03 ATI col, s13.10.03, Miami Leasing Inc r22.03.04, s24.04.04 str; Arrow Air s03.07.05; sMIA new green/blue col, sis Cairo-Mildenhall 16.02.06 (for sale by 05.06), str Miami presum ar 06-07, presum scrapped by 11.09

N774FT / Wien Alaska livery — Photo Jacques Barbé

N906R / Air Transport International / Amsterdam

N906R / Emery — via E.J.Gual

46112/520   N776FT
63CF   mfd 27.01.1970

N866F ONA 07.04.70, named "Sovereign"; Seaboard World AL lsd 24.20.73; ONA ret 21.12.73; lsd again 14.10.74; Cargolux slsd 10.12.74; Seaboard ret 03.07.75, lsd again 01.08.75, ret 14.05.76; ONA ret 15.05.76; Seaboard World AL lsd 20.12.77; **TF-FLF** Loftleidir Icelandic slsd 09.05.78; **N866F** Seaboard World AL ret 09.10.78; TF-FLF Loftleidir Icelandic slsd 01.04.79; N866F Seaboard World AL ret 12.79; Saudia slsd 21.12.79; Seaboard World AL ret 02.80; **TF-FLF** Icelandair slsd 22.02.80; Nigeria AW slsd 09.80; **N776FT** Flying Tiger Line ret 20.11.80; **TF-FLF** Icelandair lsd 12.80; **N776FT** Flying Tiger Line ret 01.81; Air India lsd 29.01.81; Air India Cargo titles, fuselage all white, sisJFK 27.07.81; Flying Tiger Line ret 16.08.81; cvtd to DC8-73CF 09.84; United Parcel Svc-UPS 30.09.84; **N812UP** United Parcel Svc-UPS rr 01.85; s10.10.03 Cleveland nc, type wfu by 12.05.09, s23.09.09, UPS to Aersale 01.11.10, canc 01.01.11 (?) pwfu ROW

N866F ▧ *Overseas National Airways* ▧ *London Gatwick* ▧
1977   *Coll. Guy Van Herbruggen*

TF-FLF ▧ *Loftleidir Icelandic*

N776FT ▧ *Air India, Icelandair c/s* ▧ *Paris Orly*

N776FT / *Flying Tigers*

N776FT / *Flying Tigers, after -73CF conversion* / *1984* / *Atlanta*

46049/479   N778FT
63CF   mfd 30.06.1969

N8639 Seaboard World AL 08.08.69; Loftleidir Icelandic lsd 27.05.70 named "Torfinnur Karlefni"; ret 01.10.70 / lsd 18.05.71, ret 01.09.71 / lsd 01.05.71, ret 01.09.72 / lsd 01.05.73, ret 25.01.74 ; Cargolux lsd 26.10.74; Seaboard ret 11.12.74; Loftleidir Icelandic lsd 16.12.75; Seaboard ret 15.01.76; Saudia lsd 01.06.77; Seaboard ret 05.79; **TF-FLC** Greyhound Lsg & Financial 14.05.79; Seaboard World AL lsd 14.05.79; Flugleidir slsd 14.05.79; Nigeria AW slsd 09.79; Flugleidir ret 10.79; Saudia slsd 11.79; Flugleidir ret 07.12.79; Cargolux slsd 12.79; Flugleidir ret 10.80; Air India slsd 01.12.80; **N778FT** Flying Tiger Line ret 02.81; ONA lsd 01.03.81; Icelandair slsd 01.03.81; Saudia slsd 01.03.81; **TF-FLC** Saudia rr 05.81, in full SV c/s; Icelandair ret 01.05.85; Evergreen Int'l AL lsd 02.07.85; Air India slsd 02.07.85; Air India Cargo title, sis05.86 Frankfurt; Icelandair ret 25.07.86; Saudia slsd 25.07.86; Icelandair ret 06.87;

N8639   Seaboard World

N8639   Seaboard World, in Lofleidir Icelandic c/s   1976
Coll. Guy Van Herbruggen

TF-FLC   Nigeria Airways, Saudia c/s

Tower Air 13.07.87; Chase Commercial Corp 13.07.87; **N867BX** Burlington Air Express lsd 13.07.87; own Mellon Financial 20.12.90 ; Kal-American Int'l lsd 12.91; Burlington AE 30.09.97; sold ex Mellon (!?); BAX Global AL/ATI nn 10.97; JP98, s pkd San Antonio 9.02 (str?), s str Marana 15.10.04, frd MZJ-TUS-LIM 24.02.05 for further maintenance and delivery to? s at Aeronaves hangar Lima 19.04.05 BAX fc, canc 20.12.05 to Sri Lanka; **4R-EXJ** Expo Aviation 20.12.05; sSHJ 23.02.06, sMalmö ar. 09.07, maintenance, sCGK 27.04.08, DXB 18.01.12; Fits Air nn ar 05.13; based at MLA since 01.2013, to be wfu in 2014, replaced by MD-80Fs

N867BX / Burlington Air Express

4R-EXJ / Expo Air

46140/528   N797FT
63CF   mfd 01.04.1970

N124AF American Flyers AL 19.05.70; Universal AL mgd 25.05.71; **N797FT** Flying Tiger Line 04.06.71; Trans International AL lsd 01.06.72; Flying Tiger ret 30.03.73; Cargolux lsd 11.05.77; Loftleidir Icelandic slsd 11.05.77; Cargolux ret 01.09.77; Flying Tiger Line ret 15.09.77; own ONA 08.05.81; Pacific East Air slsd 07.06.82; Flying Tiger Line ret 23.09.83; dam 25.10.83 when landed long in windshear conditions, left the runway, and slid into a swamp; repaired; cvtd to DC-8-73CF 05.84; United Parcel Svc-UPS 18.05.84; **N840UP** United Parcel Svc-UPS rr 06.84; type wfu by 12.05.09, sROW 13.11.09, UPS to Aersale Inc 29.12.10, canc 24.03.11 pwfu ROW

N124AF   American Flyers Airline   Brussels

N797FT   Trans International

N797FT / Loftleidir Icelandic, Flying Tiger Line cheatline

N797FT / Pacific East Air

N797FT — Flying Tigers — Brussels

N797FT — Photo NTSB

Accident description

The DC-8 departed New York on a ferry flight to NAS Chambers. There it was to convert to a military charter cargo flight to Keflavik. The captain flew the ground controlled approach (GCA) instrument approach about 15 knots above the proper reference speed to compensate for a pilot report of the existence of windshear near the runway threshold. The airplane crossed the threshold of runway 10 about ten knots above reference speed and landed between 3,100 and 3,800 feet beyond the runway threshold. Runway 10 was 8,068 feet long. The flightcrew was unable to stop the airplane on the runway. The airplane went off the side of the runway and slid into a swamp at the end of the runway.

PROBABLE CAUSE: "The National Transportation Safety Board determines that the probable cause of this accident was the flightcrew's mismanagement of the airplane's airspeed, resulting in an excessively long landing on a wet, partially flooded runway; mismanagement of thrust reversers; and hydroplaning. Contributing to this accident was the failure of airport management to identify, assess, and disseminate hazardous runway conditions warnings and the failure of air traffic controllers to inform the flight crew that there was standing water on the runway."

46108/522   N798FT
63CF   mfd 05.02.1970

N123AF American Flyers AL 24.04.70; Universal AL mgd 25.05.71; Flying Tiger Line 04.06.71; Trans International AL lsd 04.06.71; **N798FT** Flying Tiger Line ret 17.09.71; Trans International AL lsd 15.12.71; Flying Tiger Line ret 15.09.72; own ARMCO Industrial 12.79; own ONA 04.81; cvtd to DC8-73CF 07.84; United Parcel Svc-UPS 05.07.84; **N818UP** United Parcel Svc-UPS rr 10.84; sROW 23.04.09, UPS to Aersale Inc 30.11.10, canc 27.12.10 pwfu ROW, sROW 07.10.11 wfu

N798FT / Flying Tigers / Los Angeles 16.11.72   Coll. Jacques Guillem via John Wegg

N818UP / United Parcel Service

 **46001/395** N799FT
63CF mfd 19.08.1968

N863F Air Siam Hong Kong

N863F Overseas National Airways London Gatwick 1972

N863F ONA 23.09.68 named "Triumphant"; Air Siam lsd 28.03.71 in mixed pax/cargo config; ONA ret 31.01.72; **N799FT** Flying Tiger Line 17.09.73; **HB-IDM** SATA 18.06.74 named "Ville de Carouge"; Air Afrique lsd 11.75; SATA ret 01.76; Trans International AL lsd 14.12.78; **N872TV** Trans International AL bt 03.03.79; Transamerica AL nn 01.10.79; Air Afrique lsd 08.82; Transamerica AL ret 17.09.82; cvtd to DC8-73CF 03.84; United Parcel Svc-UPS lsd 12.11.86; Transamerica ret 24.12.86; **EI-BTG** GPA Group 01.87; Flying Tiger Line lsd 01.02.87; **N706FT** Flying Tiger Line lsd 19.07.87; own Transtiger Corp; own Chrysler AMC 16.09.88; Federal Express mgd; **N404FE** Federal Express rr 20.02.90; United Parcel Svc-UPS 30.07.90; **N810UP** United Parcel Svc-UPS rr 09.90; type wfu by 12.05.09, sROW 13.11.09, UPS to Aersale Inc 30.09.10, canc 18.10.10 pwfu

N799FT / Flying Tiger Line, Air Siam basic livery / Narita / 1972 — Collection Jacques Guillem via John Wegg

EI-BTG / Flying Tigers / Milan Malpensa

N706FT small Federal Express sticker, FTL basic livery — via E.J.Gual

N404FE small Federal Express sticker, FTL basic livery — Zürich Kloten

46088/464   N865F
63CF   mfd 04.1969

N865F ONA 29.05.69 named "Superb"; **OE-IBO** Austrian Air Transport lsd 24.09.73; **N865F** ONA ret 05.12.74; Seaboard World AL lsd 30.01.75; Cargolux slsd 13.03.76; Seaboard ret 01.06.77; ONA ret 01.06.77; Seaboard World AL 20.10.77; **TF-FLC** Loftleidir Icelandic lsd 28.10.78; Air India slsd 01.79; Nigeria AW slsd 03.79; Seaboard ret 01.04.79; Flugleidir lsd 01.04.79; **N865F** Saudia slsd 14.05.79; Flying Tiger Line ret 30.04.81; ONA lsd 23.06.81; Saudia slsd 06.81; own Wells Fargo Bank 02.82; ONA ret 06.83; Air India slsd 09.83; to ATASCO Leasing 03.84; Emery WW lsd 07.84; own EDS Financial Corp 17.12.85; SSB&TC r28.09.99, FSB r06.01.00; Murray Avtn s13.01.01; sDetroit YIP white, id s2.09.01, s05.01.03, s22.05.03 (is??), s12.12.03 Cleveland in svc white, s28.02.04 Ostend, titles; National AL nn 12.08; WFBN, National Air Cargo Group 30.12.08, s SNN 25.07.09 National AL titles, ex Murray col, sis MIA 06.10, wfu of type 31.05.12, donated to Yankee Air Force Museum YIP 29.06.12, filed 28.12.12, r14.01.13, presum for display at Willow Run (current location since 06.12 not repo), s wfu YIP 26.02.13, Yankee Air Force sold to Global Aviation Leasing LLC 24.10.12, filed 10.06.13, r19.08.13, to be scrapped, worth $30.000, to use that money for the museum, sDetroit YIP 26.08.14 white repo being prepared for new operator, perhaps in South Pacific region

OE-IBO // *Austrian*

TF-FLC // *Nigeria Airways, Loftleidir Icelandic basic livery* // *Lyon–Saint-Exupéry (Satolas)* // *1979*

N865F // *Air India Cargo, Saudia basic livery* // *Paris CDG* // *August 1980*

45968/389 N871TV
63CF mfd 29.07.1968

N4908C Capitol Int'l AW 29.08.68; intended as N908CL but NTU; Flying Tiger Line 29.09.75; **HB-IDS** SATA 30.09.75 named "Ville de Lausanne"; **N871TV** Flying Tiger Line 18.02.78; Trans International AL lsd 10.04.79; Transamerica AL nn 01.10.79; Flying Tiger ret 26.05.80; lsd again 10.09.80, ret 01.07.84; cvtd to DC8-73CF 08.84; United Parcel Svc-UPS 14.09.84; **N868UP** United Parcel Svc-UPS rr 11.84; type wfu by 12.05.09, frd SDF-ROW 14.05.09, s25.08.09, UPS to Aersale 31.03.11, canc 03.08.11

N4908C Capitol London Gatwick

N871TV Flying Tigers, SATA basic cheatline

N871TV / Flying Tigers, Trans International livery / Atlanta August 1980 — Collection Jacques Guillem, via John Wegg

N868UP / United Parcel Service — via E.J.Gual

✈ 46117/525　　N701FT
63CF　　　　　　　mfd 02.03.1970

N4869T Trans International AL 15.05.70; Transamerica AL nn 01.10.79; Air Afrique lsd 10.79 for Hadj; Transamerica ret 11.79; lsd again 30.08.82; Transamerica AL ret 09.82; cvtd DC-8-73CF 06.84; United Parcel Svc-UPS lsd 27.10.86; Transamerica ret 24.12.86, GPA 01.87, Spectrum Capital 01.87, Transtiger Corp 01.87; Flying Tiger Line lsd 22.01.87; **N701FT** Flying Tiger Line rr 04.88; own First Fidelity Bank 30.09.88; Federal Express mgd 07.08.89; **N401FE** Federal Express rr 08.01.90; United Parcel Svc-UPS 17.09.90; **N805UP** United Parcel Svc-UPS rr 10.90; type wfu by 12.05.09, s str ROW 29.07.09, Aersale 28.01.10, canc 06.05.10 pwfu ROW

N4869T　Transamerica

N4869T　Flying Tigers　Pinal Airpark (Marana)　　　　　　via E.J. Gual

N701FT / Flying Tigers

N401FE / small Federal Express sticker near door 1L, FTL basic livery

46073/485 N702FT
63CF mfd **31.07.1969**

N4865T Trans International AL 22.08.69; Aeronaves de Mexico lsd 17.03.71, named "Chiapas"; Trans International ret 30.03.74; Air Algérie lsd 11.75; Trans International ret 01.76; Air Afrique lsd 10.79; Transamerica ret 11.79, lsd again 20.09.80, ret 11.80; cvtd to DC8-73CF 07.82; United Parcel Svc-UPS lsd 07.11.86; Transamerica ret 24.12.86, GPA 01.87, Spectrum Capital 01.87, Transtiger Corp 01.87; Flying Tiger Line lsd 01.87; own First Fidelity Bank 30.09.88; **N702FT** Flying Tiger Line rr 06.89; Federal Express mgd 07.08.89; **N402FE** Federal Express rr 01.01.90; United Parcel Svc-UPS 17.09.90; **N803UP** United Parcel Svc-UPS rr 11.90; frd 21.08.08 to ROW, str, sis 13.02.09, type wfu by 12.05.09, sROW 23.09.09; **N155CA** National AL lsd 04.12.09; frd ROW-OSC 06.12.09, rr 31.12.09, first svc YIP-CPH 09.01.10 basic new UPS col, new reg on sticker, UPS to AerSale 26.02.10 r01.03.10, lse to National continues, sis LUX 11.03.10, sis OST 31.05.12! frd ABQ-ROW 31.05.12 for str/wfu, s16.01.15 wfu

N4865T Trans International

N4865T Transamerica 09.09.80 Coll. Guy Van Herbruggen

N4865T Flying Tigers 1988

via E.J.Gual

N402FE / small Federal Express sticker near door 1L, FTL basic livery - Frankfurt am Main

N803UP / United Parcel Service   via E.J.Gual

N155CA / National Airlines

46059/456 N703FT
63C mfd 31.03.1969

N4864T Trans International AL 25.04.69; Air Afrique lsd 05.79; Transamerica AL ret 11.79; ONA lsd 09.06.81; Saudia slsd 06.81; Transamerica ret 19.11.81; Evergreen Int'l AL lsd 12.12.81; Transamerica ret 31.12.84; cvtd to DC-8-73CF 02.85; Spirit of America AL lsd 08.85; Transamerica ret 09.86; United Parcel Svc-UPS lsd 17.10.86; Transamerica ret 24.12.86; GPA 01.87; Spectrum Capital 01.87; Transtiger Corp 01.87; Flying Tiger Line lsd 01.02.87; **N703FT** Flying Tigers rr 07.88; own Pacificcorp 30.09.88 ; **N403FE** Federal Express mgd 07.08.89; own UPS 29.06.90, op basic Flying Tiger col, small Federal Express sticker; **N813UP** United Parcel Svc-UPS ret 07.01.91; rr 02.91, sis EMA 23.04.97, frd MHT-ROW 30.12.08, str, UPS to Aersale Inc 30.11.10, canc 27.12.10 pwfu.

N4864T — Trans International — London Gatwick

N4864T — Transamerica

N4864T — Flying Tigers

via E.J.Gual

N703FT / Flying Tigers / Los Angeles

N703FT / small Federal Express sticker near door 1R, FTL basic livery

46090/504   N705FT
63CF   mfd 11.1969

N4867T Trans International AL 29.12.69; UTA lsd 08.72; Trans International ret 12.72; Air Afrique lsd 11.74; Trans International ret 12.74; lsd 09.75, ret 11.75; lsd 09.76, ret 11.76; Transamerica AL nn 01.10.79; cvtd 03.83; Spirit of America AL lsd 04.85; Transamerica ret 09.86; United Parcel Svc-UPS lsd 05.12.86; Transamerica ret 24.12.86, GPA 01.02.87, Transtiger Corp 01.02.87; Flying Tiger Line lsd 01.02.87; **N705FT** Flying Tiger Line rr 06.88; own Pacificorp 30.09.88; Federal Express mgd 07.08.89; **N405FE** Federal Express rr 20.02.90; own UPS 29.06.90; **N814UP** United Parcel Svc-UPS ret 07.01.91; rr 03.91, type wfu by 12.05.09, s23.09.09, UPS to AerSale 26.02.10, r30.03.10, canc 18.09.14

N4867T — Union de Transports Aériens, Trans International livery — Paris Le Bourget — 1972

N4867T — Air Afrique, Trans International livery — 1974

N4867T / Flying Tigers / Miami

via E.J.Gual

N706FT / Flying Tigers / Frankfurt am Main

46089/501   N707FT
63CF   mfd 20.10.1969–

N4866T Trans International AL 29.12.69; Aeronaves de Mexico lsd 13.03.71, name "Veracruz"; Aeromexico nn 02.72; Trans International ret 30.03.74; Transamerica AL nn 01.10.79; Air Afrique lsd 10.79 for Hadj; Transamerica ret 11.79; lsd again 09.80; Transamerica AL ret 11.80; cvtd 12.82; Spirit of America AL lsd 01.05.85; Transamerica ret 09.86; United Parcel Svc-UPS lsd 20.11.86; Transamerica ret 24.12.86, GPA 03.87, Transtiger Corp 03.87; Flying Tiger Line lsd 03.87; **N707FT** Flying Tiger Line rr 06.88; own Chrysler AMC 09.02.89; Federal Express mgd 07.08.89; sis Zurich 17.09.89, Flying Tigers basic c/s, no titles; **N407FE** Federal Express rr 28.12.89; United Parcel Svc-UPS 30.07.90; **N811UP** United Parcel Svc-UPS rr 11.90; frd SDF-ROW 26.02.09, UPS to Aersale 01.11.10, canc 11.01.11 pwfu ROW, s28.04.13 wfu

N4866T Aeronaves de Mexico, named "Veracruz" Paris Le Bourget 1971

N4866T Aeromexico London Gatwick

N4866T / Transamerica Spirit of America

N4866T / Flying Tigers

via E.J.Gual

Memory Lane

Peter Okicich, Flying Tiger Line

I was a check captain assigned to the FTL DC-8-63 simulator instruction and was conducting a check ride for a crew. We were pretty casual then as the LAX base was virtually empty on the weekends. I was preparing to simulate a loss of hydraulic fluid that would require the engineer's input and then set up the captain for an abnormal flap landing. Coordinating with check-engineer we simulated a loss of hydraulic pressure. At that very moment there was a serious odour of hydraulic fluid and I commented on how realistic the exercise seemed.
At that moment, I swivelled in my seat to look out the rear window at our terrain map we used to give heading commands and guidance for approaches. I immediately noticed that the actual simulator was level and had settled down as if unpowered. I stopped the exercise and exited the simulator when I immediately noticed a lake of hydraulic fluid in the bottom of the simulator bay.
My concern for the crew, who would have to delay their departure for home, because the check ride was incomplete, was foremost in my mind. I contacted the simulator technician on duty and we discovered an actual busted hydraulic line. We found another hydraulic line, about six feet longer than necessary. Tony Fiorelli, who is still a member of FTLPA, cleaned up the spilled hydraulic fluid and affixed the newer hydraulic line. We found a huge barrel of hydraulic fluid in a nearby hanger. I borrowed a idle forklift from the hanger and brought the barrel of hydro to the simulator bay where we used a hand-cranked pump to transfer the fluid.

After all the mess was cleaned up, we repowered the simulator, repositioned the aircraft, and completed the check ride. The crew passed with flying colours and was released to travel home. All of us "volunteers" - stained with hydraulic fluid on our clothes and shoes - took about seven hours for a normal four-hour period.
I never got in trouble with the union for using the forklift without authorisation and this whole exercise of "can-do spirit" exemplifies why the Flying Tigers were such a great family.

In 1968 I was a baby-faced co-pilot on the DC-8 flying a load of passengers from Travis AFB to Anchorage Alaska. As fate would have it, my wife's first flight as a newly hired Flight Attendant would be this same flight. We hit it off and have been together since, forty six years.

Memory Lane

Paul Rebscher, Flying Tiger Line

I flew on the DC-8 as an engineer from 1971 to 1980, mostly international. The "oiler" on the Eight was the operator of a full panel with all systems displayed and was the operator of these various systems. Upon takeoff the pressurisation was controlled by two levers just to the left of the engineer's panel. These two levers were called the "lollypops" and required the engineer to grab them and try and control the rate of pressurisation as the aircraft ascended. If done properly there would be no chatter or bumps that could be heard or felt by those in the cockpit.

REBSCHER, Harold Paul

Many times when not done the right way, the Captain would turn around and shout, DON'T YOU KNOW HOW TO DO YOUR JOB! and of course for a new engineer this was very embarrassing. Also, the engineer on the freighter was the cook and had to warm up the meals in the galley, and one time as I removed them from the oven I dropped the Captain's steak on the deck and had to inform him that I had dropped his meal, to which he replied, NO SON YOU DROPPED YOURS! - so guess who went without a meal. The Eight was a great airplane and carried a big payload compared to other aircraft Tigers had. I enjoyed my time on the Eight a lot.

5 FLIGHTDECK

In comparison to the Boeing 707 aircraft, the DC-8 cockpit is very spacious and is a three-person cockpit. It accommodates a standard crew of a captain, first officer, flight engineer and a supernumerary or jumpseat if required. The overwater intercontinental aircraft was also equipped with a navigator's station behind the captain's seat. The navigator position was removed in the late 60's to become an additional jumpseat seat. Like all aircraft of its generation, the DC-8 includes a large number of functional switches and levers. The instrumentation and layout are typical for the type, although not necessarily exact for each variant or individual aircraft. In the sixties, airlines had the opportunity to customize panel layout.

2. OBSERVER'S SEAT
4. UPPER WINDOWS
5. CLEARVIEW WINDOWS
6. FIRE EXTINGUISHING SYSTEM PANEL
7. OVER HEAD SWITCH PANEL
8. GLARESHIELD INSTRUMENT PANEL
9. CAPTAINS FLIGHT INSTRUMENT PANEL
10. CAPTAIN'S SEAT
11. ENGINE INSTRUMENT PANEL
12. PILOTS' CONTROL PEDESTAL
13. FIRST OFFICER'S FLIGHT INSTRUMENT PANEL
14. FIRST OFFICER'S SEAT
15. SYSTEMS ENGINEER'S SEAT
16. SYSTEMS ENGINEER'S CONTROL PEDESTAL
17. SYSTEMS ENGINEER'S CONTROL PANEL

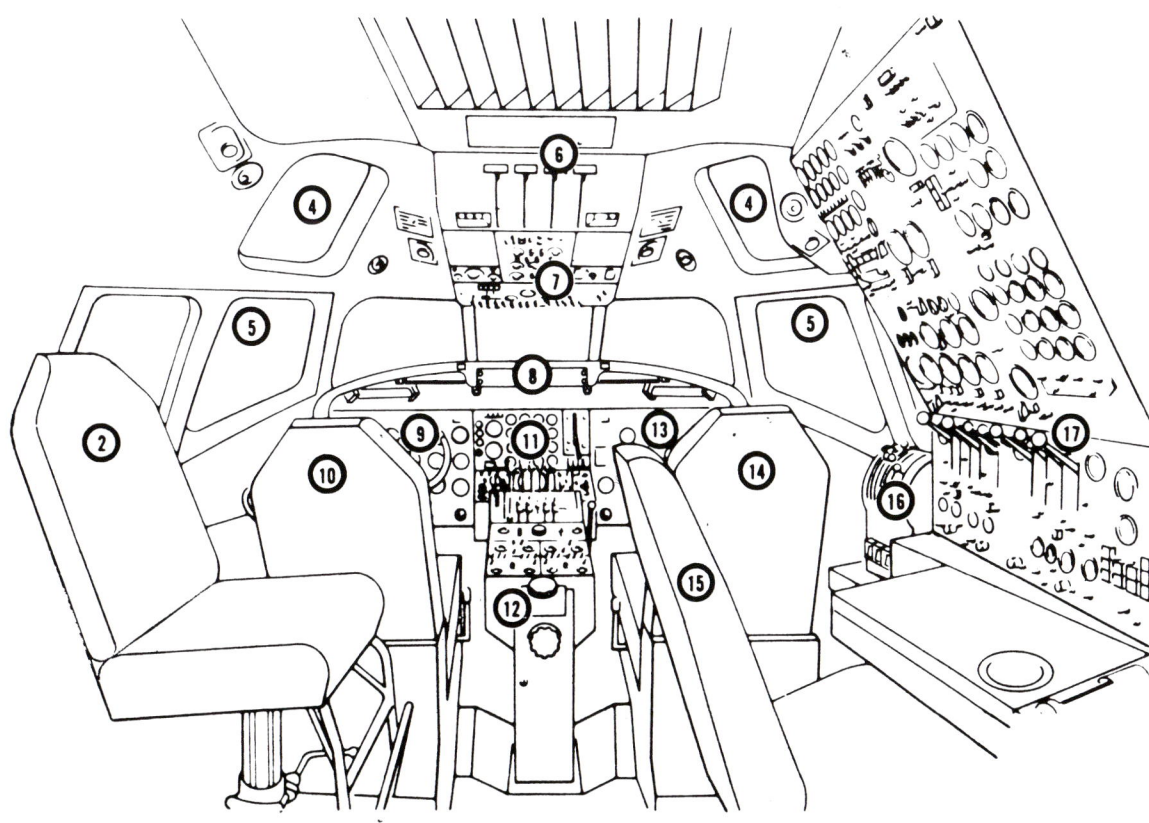

Typical flight compartment arrangement

Cargolux DC-8-63AF LX-ACV ◥ *formerly N779FT with Flying Tigers* Photo Michel Anciaux

DC-8-63 Flying Tigers flight simulator cockpit

DC-8-55CF Jet Trader Loftleidir TF-LLK ◥ *ex Seaboard N802SW*

Flight instruments are duplicated on the captain's and first officer's sides. Engine instruments are shared in the centre panel.

Cargolux DC-8-63AF LX-ACV / formerly N779FT with Flying Tigers

Photo Michel Anciaux

The wheel on the far left side of the flight station is the command steering control, which is used on the ground for increased travel of the nose gear.

The parking brake is controlled by the PARK BRAKE-PULL TO ENGAGE knob in the centre of the nose gear steering wheel.

Captain's panel

1. Ground speed indicator (deactivated in picture)
2. Airspeed indicator (ASI)
3. Flaps limiting airspeed panel
4. Captain's oxygen regulator panel
5. True airspeed indicator (TAS)
6. Gyro compass indicator
7. Horizon flight director indicator
8. Horizontal situation indicator (HSI) – course indicator
9. Comparator (annunciator fail lights)
10. Altimeter
11. Radio altimeter
12. Vertical speed indicator (VSI)
13. Clock
14. DME indicator (distance measuring equipment)
15. Turn & bank indicator
16. Autopilot servo indicators (aileron, elevator and rudder)
17. Flight director mode annunciator

First Officer's panel

18. Comparator (annunciator fail lights)
19. Airplane overspeed warning indicator
20. True airspeed (TAS)
21. Autopilot status indicator and trim indicators
22. Elevator position indicator
23. Flap position indicator
24. Marker lights (outer, middle and inner)
25. Flaps limiting airspeed panel
26. First Officer oxygen regulator panel

Glare shield panel

Centre panel

27. Flight director control panel
28. Altitude alert director
29. Compass mirror
30. Emergency air brake handle
31. Standby attitude indicator
32. Ram air temperature/engine pressure ratio (EPR) indicator
33. Low oil pressure lights
34. Engine Pressure Ratio (EPR) gauge
35. Engine exhaust gas temperature (EGT) gauge
36. Engine tachometer (N1 RPM gauge)
37. Fuel flow gauges
38. Gear test light switch
39. Gear door warning lights
40. Landing gear lever

Overhead switch panel

41. Voice recorder system
42. HF-1/HF-2 control panel
43. Weather radar control panel
44. Compass controller
45. ADF control panel
46. ATC transponder control panel
47. Navigation instrument switching panel
48. SELCAL (selective calling) control panel
49. Engine starter switches
50. Engine igniter switches
51. Stall warning test switch
52. Exterior lighting switches
53. No smoking & seatbelt sign switches
54. Pitot heat switch and selector

Overhead fire shutoff and agent discharge controls

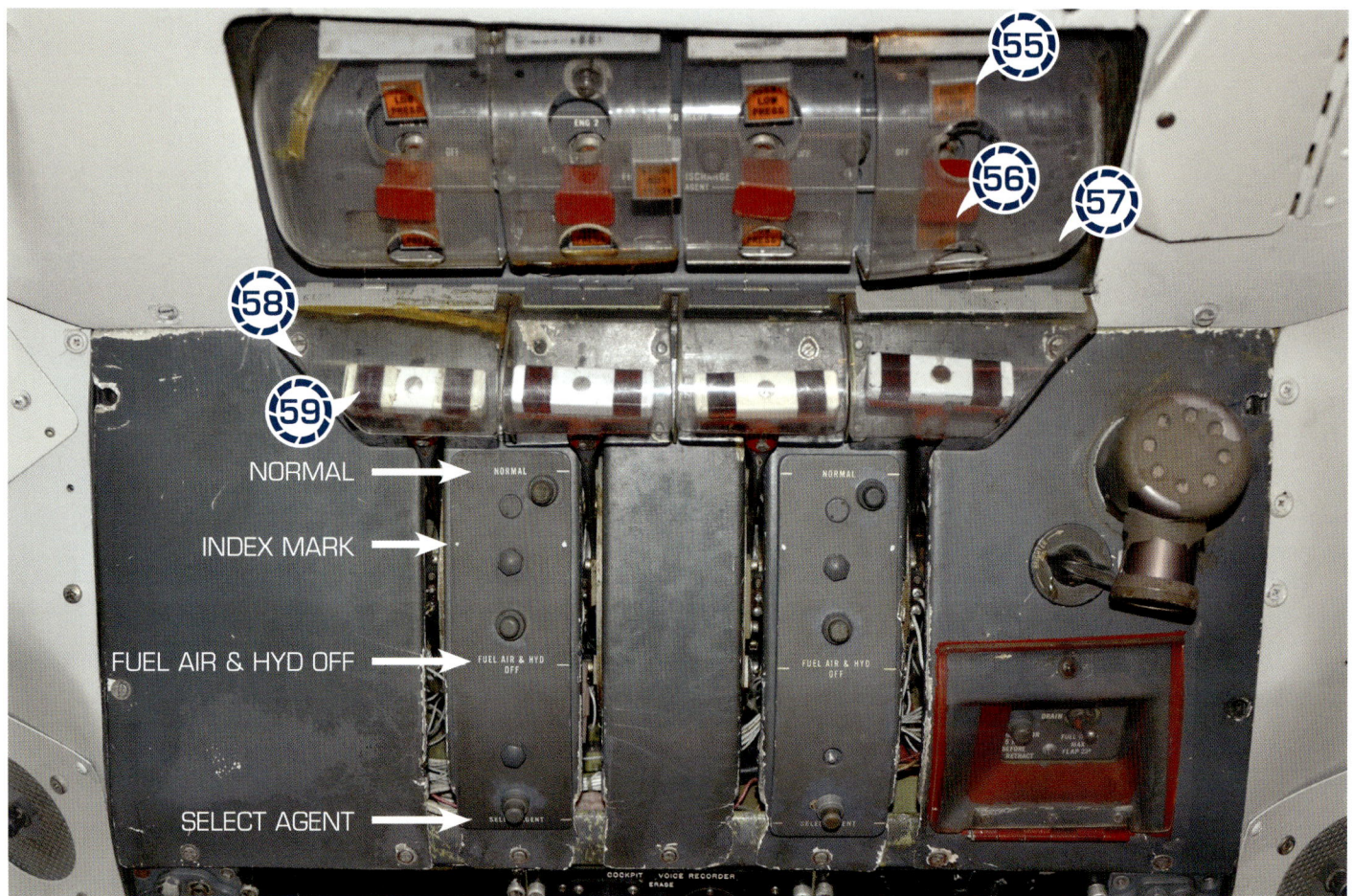

55. Agent low pressure light
56. Fire extinguishing agent discharge switch
57. Cover
58. Fire shutoff lever guard
59. Fire shutoff lever
    - in NORMAL position (all valves open, agent handle cover closed)
    - at INDEX MARK (ground check generator field open, low pressure pneumatic system off)
    - at FUEL AIR & HYD OFF position (fuel, hydraulic and pneumatic valves closed)
    - in SELECT AGENT, the agent discharge switch is fully opent

Pilot's control pedestal

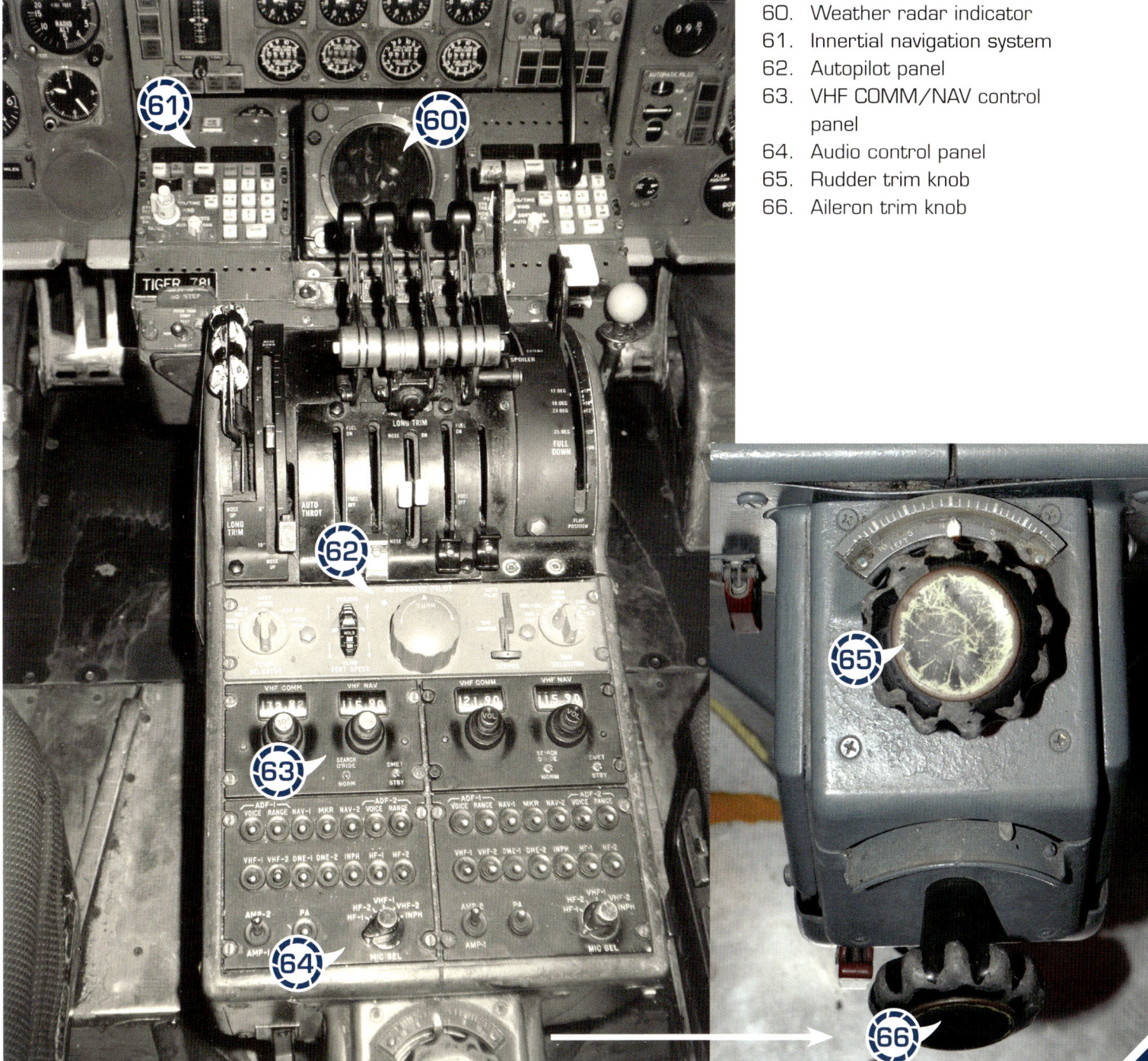

60. Weather radar indicator
61. Innertial navigation system
62. Autopilot panel
63. VHF COMM/NAV control panel
64. Audio control panel
65. Rudder trim knob
66. Aileron trim knob

Pedestal of "Tiger" N781FT

Throttle quadrant panel

67. Reverser levers
68. Reverser bucket/door indicators
69. Spoiler lever
70. Throttle levers
71. Fuel shut-off levers
72. Flap lever
73. Autothrottle switch
74. Elevator trim indicator
75. Elevator trim lever
76. Control surface lock lever

Flight Engineer's panel

(or Systems Engineer's panel)

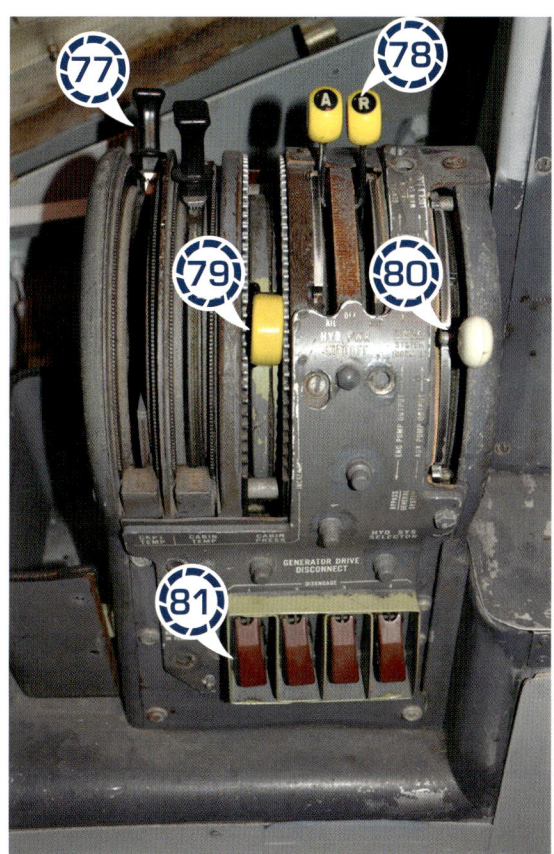

77. Cabin temperature setting levers
78. Aileron and rudder hydraulic levers
79. Cabin pressure lever
80. Hydraulic pump lever
81. Generator disconnect switches

Electrical control panel

82. Master battery switch
83. Generator load (DC) gauges
84. Generator temperature gauges
85. Generator warning annunciators
86. Generator load (AC) gauges
87. Generator switches
88. Bus fail annunciators
89. Emergency bus power switches
90. System switch and annunciator
91. Passenger oxygen venting and supply switch
92. Cockpit flight recorder switch
93. Fire test switches
94. Fire/smoke detector test system
95. Hydraulic system gauges
96. Main gear spoiler test
97. Hydraulic control switches

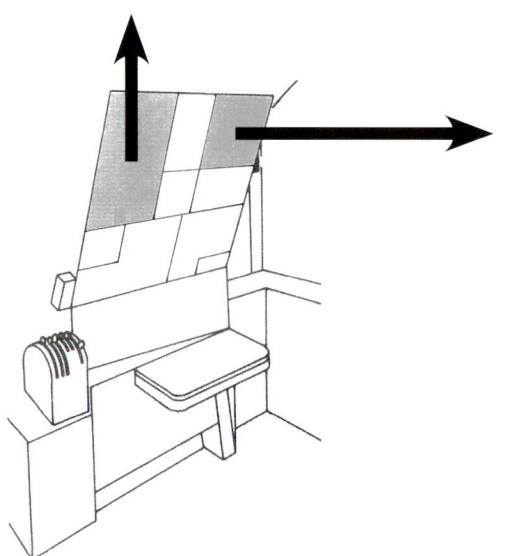

Fire warning & Hydraulics panel

Engine and de-icing control panels

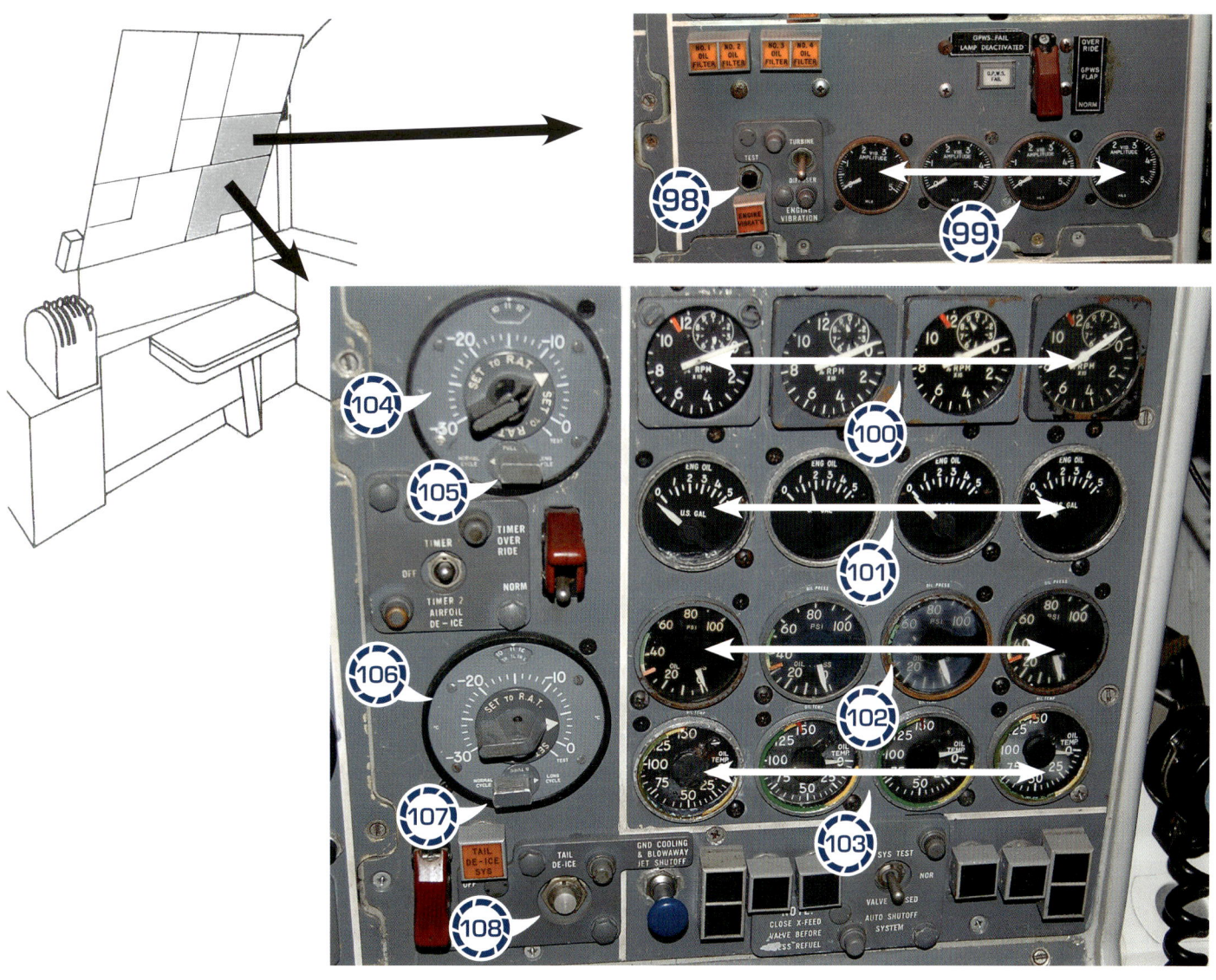

98. Engine vibration warning light and test
99. Engine vibration monitor gauges
100. N1 RPM gauges
101. Engine oil quantity gauges
102. Engine oil pressure gauges
103. Engine oil temp gauges
104. Engine temperature setting control
105. Engine auto/manual switch
106. Airframe temp setting control
107. Airframe auto/manual switch
108. Tail surface de-icing switch and test

Refrigeration, air conditioning, pressurization & pneumatic system panels

109. Freon saturation and superheat temperature indicators
110. Freon compressor switches and (operating & overheat) indicating lights
111. Recirculating fan control switches
112. Cockpit & cabin temperature control knobs
113. Cabin air temperature indicator
114. Cabin pressure controller
115. Cabin altitude and differential-pressure indicator
116. Cabin rate-of-climb indicator
117. Cabin compressor RPM indicator
118. Cabin compressor switches
119. Pneumatic shutoff switches
120. Pneumatic manifold dual air temp indicator
121. Pneumatic manifold air over temperature warning lights
122. Pneumatic manifold air pressure indicator
123. Skid control monitor
124. Flight engineers lights control panel

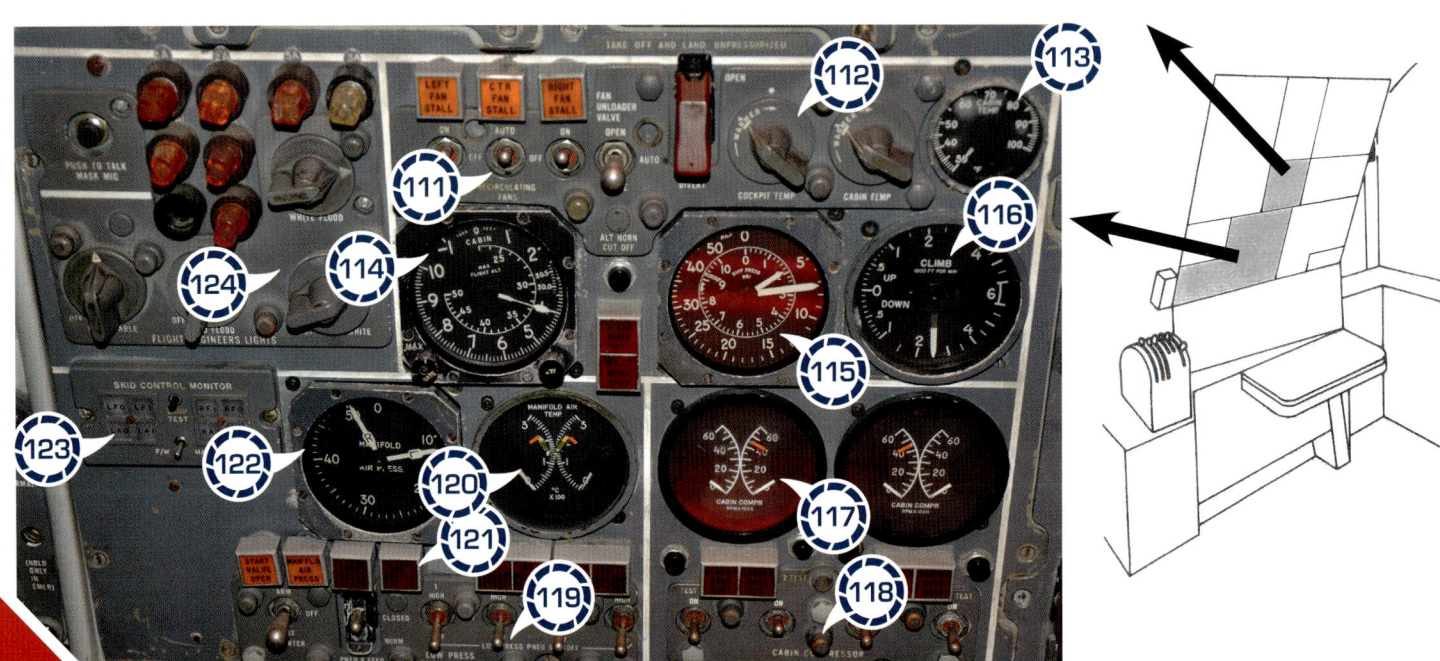

Fuel systems – controls & indicators panel

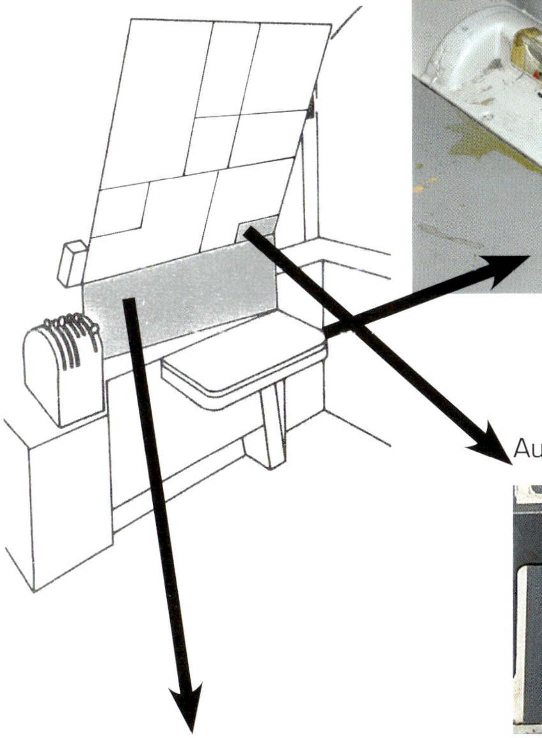

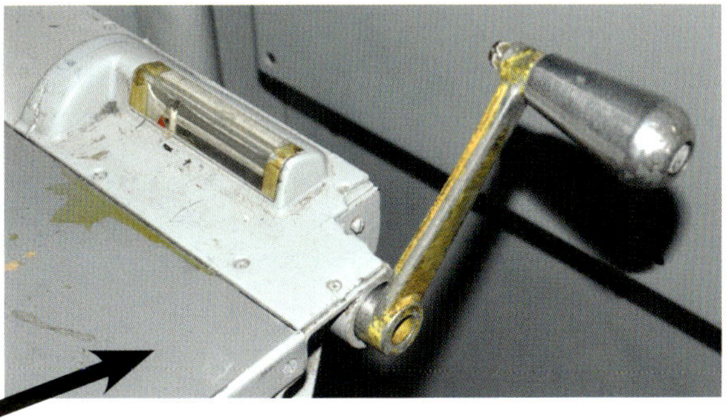

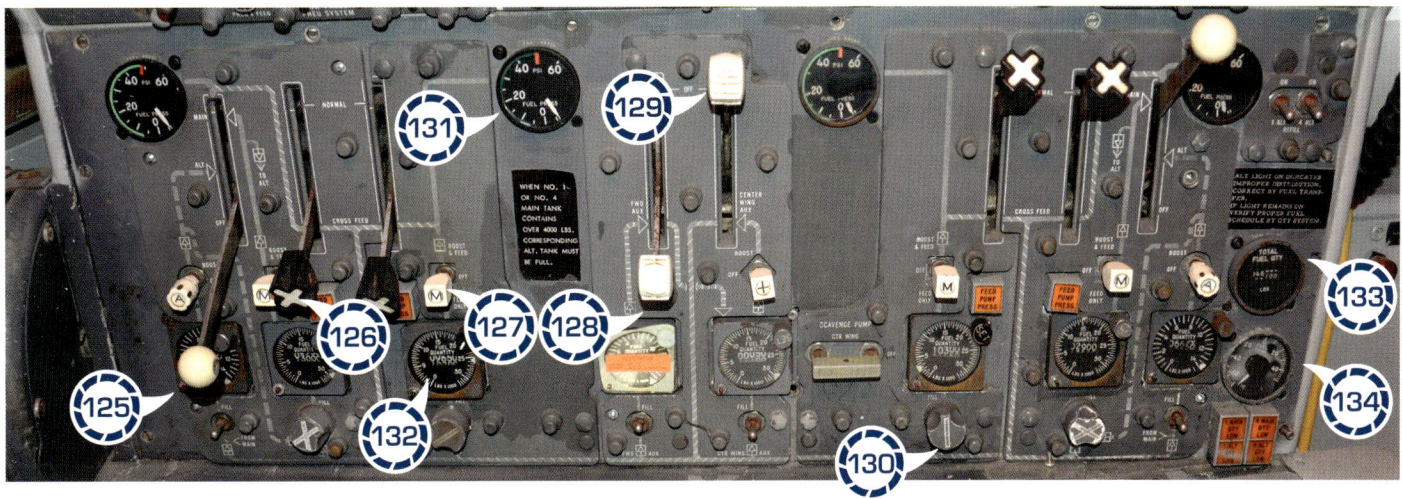

At the right corner of the Flight Engineer's table is the Fuel dump handcrank used to operate the fuel dump mechanically.

57 counter clockwise rotation is required to extend chutes.

Auto shutoff system

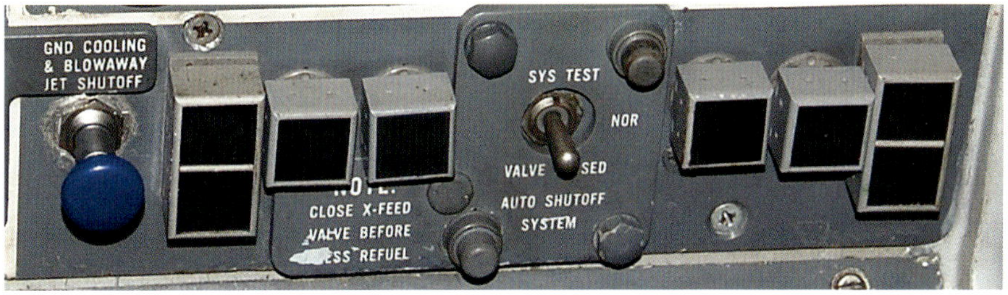

125. Tank selector lever
126. Cross-feed levers
127. Boost (& feed) pump switches
128. Forward auxiliary selector lever
129. Centre wing auxiliary selector lever
130. Tank fill valve switches
131. Fuel pressure gauge
132. Fuel quantity indicator
133. Total fuel quantity indicator
134. Fuel temperature indicator

Circuit breakers panels

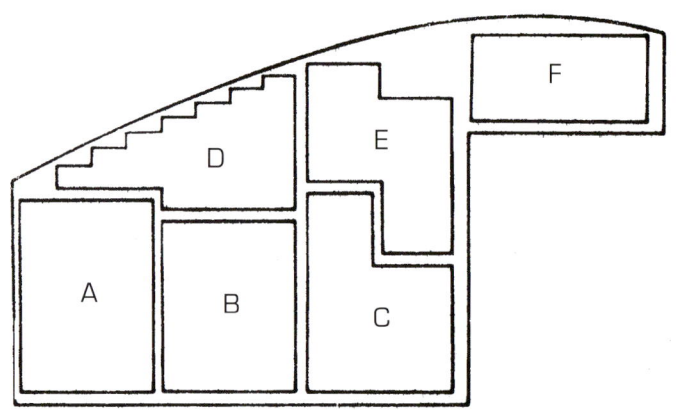

A. DC buses panel
B. BAC buses panel
C. Generator buses, AC Emergency buses and Cabin buses
D. AC buses, lighting secondary and instrument secondary
E. Radio buses and battery bus
F. Radio buses
G. Radio rack circuit breaker/fuse panel

6 THE FLYING TIGERS DC-8-63 SIMULATOR

The DC-8-63 flight simulator was ordered by the Flying Tiger Line in 1967 when the airline placed its first order for ten DC-8-63F aircraft from the Douglas Aircraft Company.

The three-axis hydraulic full-motion Level A simulator was manufactured by the Link Group-Systems Division, General Precision Systems Inc., in Binghamton, New York, and Tiger took delivery at its Flight Training Center in LAX in 1968.

With this new digital technology simulator, FTL flight crews were fully trained in the operation of the DC-8-63 aircraft, minimising the actual flying time required for training. In addition, flight and operating conditions are introduced in the simulator which if encountered in actual flight would result in a major emergency; thus the crew was able to experience these conditions and perform and practice corrective actions in complete safety. Throughout a simulated flight, the operating characteristics of the simulator closely approximated those of the actual DC-8-63 aircraft. The majority of the cockpit instruments were fully activated, thus permitting instrument "flights".

The simulator's host computer system was the Link GP-4 computer. The GP-4 was a major breakthrough in first-generation digital computers and rapidly expanded aviation simulation training, making flying a whole lot safer.

In 1973, a visual display system was added to the simulator, giving both the captain and co-pilot a realistic visual representation of the scene visible from the flight deck during the take-off and approach sequences of night time operations from selected airfields and their vicinities.

The FTL DC-8-63 simulator in 1973 when the visual display system was added.

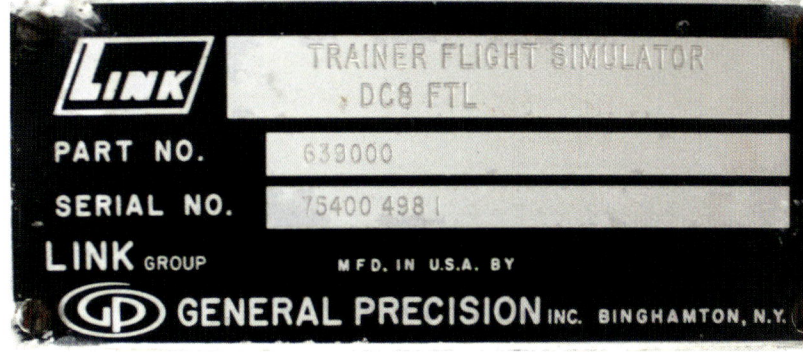

Construction plate of the FTL DC-8-63 flight simulator

Memory Lane

by Captain John Dickson, FedEx Express

I consider myself one of the luckiest aviators alive since the Flying Tiger Line hired me as crewmember in July of 1978. Since then my career has touched five decades. I have had the good fortune to log an enumerable amount of memories and experiences that go along with the hours I have spent in an airplane since beginning this journey as a Flight Engineer on the Douglas DC-8. In those days the Flight Engineer seat was occupied by either a very seasoned former flight mechanic, or a newly hired pilot spending some time on "the panel" before his seniority allowed upgrading to the co-pilot seat. I personally spent two years as a DC-8 F/E before moving over to the Boeing 747 in 1980.

Some of my most vivid memories come from my initial and recurrent training sessions in the DC-8 simulator, affectionately called "the box" by many of us at the time. During those years in late 1978, flight engineers were required to know a lot more about how the different systems of the aircraft operated and were interrelated with one another. Problems with a pump on one system might certainly affect how the operation of another system is conducted. After a course of training, a flight engineer became very knowledgeable in these matters. The DC-8 was not a very complicated aircraft to operate for it's time. However, by today's standards where most system operation is automatic, the Flight Engineer on a DC-8 was an extremely important part of the flight deck, their proficiency relied upon greatly by the Captain operating the aircraft.

A simulator session normally lasted a total of 4 hours with a break at the midpoint when it was brought back down to the resting position and the students and instructors exited for a coffee break. Initially all of the pilots operated as they would in the actual aircraft, going through their pre-flight flows and preparing the "plane" for flight. During training sessions there were two instructors in the simulator, one for the Captain and First Officer up front, and one for the two Flight Engineer students on the panel who would take their appropriate turns watching for alerts, lights, leaking fluids, and other tricks the instructor could throw their way.

The similar, even in those days, was extremely realistic especially for the Flight Engineer panel. Once at the simulated cruise altitude a switch could be flipped and the students in the back could be separated from the pilots up front. In this way system problems could be introduced without affecting the pilots flying their series of maneuvers up front. There were many times we would be back trying to understand and control system malfunctions while the pilots up front were flying steep turns, stalls, and touch and go's. It actually felt a little crazy and comical at times.

There isn't a Flying Tiger Second Officer (F/E) who wouldn't smile a little at the words "I smell smoke" by the instructor. This was normally met with the question, "Is it electrical?" This was a comment made by the instructor that would set the student off into a checklist of memory and written checklist directives to start flipping switches and isolating aircraft electrical system components in an attempt to identify where the smoke was being generated from. It was an extremely effective way to get to know the DC-8 electrical system and all of it's various intricacies.

The pilots up front would constantly complain about the DC-8 simulator feeling "heavier" than the actual aircraft. I never checked out as a DC-8 First Officer so I couldn't tell you. I do know that the Flight Engineer panel was as realistic as it could possibly be and was an invaluable tool in many a young pilot's career progression to the front seats.

From Los Angeles to Dayton Ohio

In 1996, the simulator was sold to Aero Service Aviation Center Inc. and moved from Los Angeles to Dayton Ohio. The first operator to lease the simulator was ATI (Air Transport International). ATI operated a total of forty-two DC-8 aircraft between 1988 and 2013 for its worldwide cargo and combi charters for the express package industry and freight forwarders, as well as for the United States Department of Defence and the automotive industry.

ATI Check Airmen and Instructor John Emlet remembers that the DC-8-63 simulator was nicknamed "The Klingon" in reference to Star Trek battlecruiser.

In 1998, the simulator started to be used by Emery Worldwide Airlines to train crew members (pilots and flight engineers) for their JT3D-equipped DC-8 fleet while the former United Airlines DC-8-71 Level C simulator (located in the same building and also owned by Aero Services) was used to train for their CFM56-equipped aircraft. African International and National Airlines crew members also conducted flight instruction in the former FTL DC-8-63 simulator.

Early 2009, the simulator was decommissioned after more than forty years of service. With the support of ATI Captain John Emlet, it was saved from being scraped and together with Justin Messenger and Steve Cannaby of Nu-Tek Aircraft Instruments who took the challenge of dismantling and moving the simulator to Augusta, KS.

ATI then moved their DC-8-60 training to Wilmington, Ohio and used the ABX DC-8-62 Level B simulator there.

After twenty-five years of DC-8 operation, ATI retired their last DC-8 in 2013, leaving only two US operators: a DC-8-63F with National Airlines and a DC-8-72 test bird with NASA. In February 2015, from the 556 DC-8 aircraft built, only fourteen (or 2.5%) are still in service, two-thirds of them in African skies.

ATI Captain John Emlet was a key contributor in saving the former FTL DC-8-63 simulator

March 2009, dismantling of the simulator is in progress. The distinctive Flying Tigers arrow was kept during the entire career of the simulator at Aero Service Photos Steve Cannaby

After a period of storage, the simulator was repainted in NASA colours with hopes to land some funding for the NASA Aviation Airborne Laboratory-themed Global Warming Learning Centre for School Children. Unfortunately, this did not find much interest and the project was scraped.

Augusta, KS   The former FTL DC-8-63 simulator on a trailer and in NASA colours   *Photos Steve Cannaby*

The Restoration Project

As a FedEx employee since 1991, Guy Van Herbruggen was always fascinated by Flying Tigers' history and its contribution to FedEx's international growth after the acquisition of Flying Tigers in 1989.

The project of bringing the former Flying Tigers DC-8 simulator to Belgium began in April 2014 when it was put on sale by its last owner, Steve Cannaby. Steve runs Nu-Tek Aircraft Instruments and is an aviation enthusiast famous for restoring and converting flight simulators. Guy met Steve in 2003 when he was restoring a Boeing 707 Link simulator for the Boeing Company that Boeing donated to the Ronald Reagan Presidential Library Foundation in Simi Valley California, as the centre piece of the Air Force One Learning Centre. Together with Peter, Charlie and Eric, the idea to acquire one of the very few remaining DC-8 simulators from across the ocean to Europe began. But who are they?

Charles Kennedy's interest in aviation started in his 70s Sydney childhood, and bloomed in the 80s after his family moved to England, necessitating a trip to Australia every other year, flying every exotic combination along the Kangaroo Route. The hobby evolved into becoming a regular features writer for Airliner World, Aviation News and Airways magazines, and piloting experience that includes flying a Piper PA-28 plus training on the 707 simulator at the Pan Am Flight Academy in Miami. His day job as a musician has created lots of international travel opportunities.

Peter Kirschen began flight training at the age of nine years old on a Link Trainer at Sabena's building at Brussels Airport. At the age of fifteen, he flew for the first time in a Saab Safir and at the age of twenty-three he took his first flying lesson in a Piper Cub. Peter joined Sabena World Airlines in 1974 where he was a DC 10 and 747 professional flight engineer from 1983 to 2001. He holds an ATPL and is a flight instructor. Peter resides in Wezembeek, Belgium and has two children.

Guy Van Herbruggen began a lifelong love of aviation when at the age of six he flew on a Sabena SE-210 Caravelle from Brussels to Tunis with his parents. Guy started to fly gliders at the age of fourteen and earned his FAA Professional Pilot IFR Multi-engine licence in 1991 followed by a flight engineer certificate with a 727 type rating. Today, Guy is an Engineering Manager at FedEx Express. He resides in Ottignies, Belgium with his wife France and their twin children, where he has restored the former Sabena Boeing 707 flight simulator built by Curtiss-Wright in 1959.

Eric Verlie's love for aviation was given to him by the baby bottle. As a kid, Grimbergen airfield near Brussels was his playground. He began his career with a private pilot licence and as a mechanic. Today Eric is CEO of Mons Saint-Ghislain airfield, CFO of the Belgian Flight School based in Charleroi, and the CEO of Aero Maintenance, an aircraft maintenance company based at Charleroi, Liège and Saint-Ghislain.

The long journey from the USA to Belgium started on August 14, 2014, when Steve Cannaby towed the former FTL simulator on a transport trailer from Augusta Kansas to Galveston Texas - a 670 mile journey - for shipping to the port of Zeebrugge in Belgium.

Loaded into vehicle carrier ship Canadian Highway, the simulator left Galveston on August 23 and, after a few ports of call to load and unload vehicles, the ship arrived in Zeebrugge, Belgium on September 22.

After destination port administration (port charges, customs clearance, brokerage fees, et al), final trucking from Zeebrugge to Saint-Ghislain airfield took place on October 6.

The short eighty-five mile journey took less than two hours. Upon arrival, offload from the flatbed truck was completed. Two months after arrival, the simulator was moved into an aircraft hangar.

Saint-Ghislain Airport (in French, Aérodrome de Saint-Ghislain) (ICAO: EBSG) is a small airfield located seven miles west of Mons in the province of Hainaut in Belgium. Privately managed, the airport has a single paved runway and is home to several flight schools, an aircraft maintenance facility, and other aeronautically-oriented leisure activities, such as aircraft restoration and amateur aircraft building. This is where Eric, Peter and Guy elected to start an aviation collection. Today the collection includes the cockpit of the first McDonnell Douglas DC-10-30CF in Europe (delivered to Sabena in 1973), a single-seat Frasca 141 trainer built in Champaign Illinois, a characteristic 'Blue Box" Link trainer, a 737-400 cockpit procedure trainer (CPT) and many other artefacts.   Photos Eric Verlie

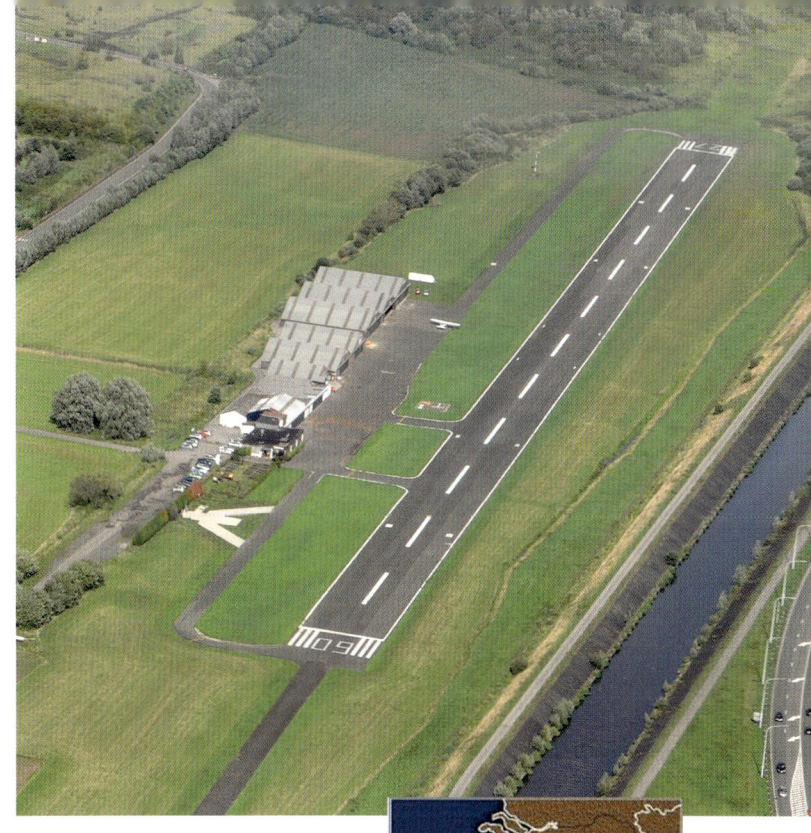

Mons (Belgium) together with Pilsen (Czech Republic) are the European Capitals of Culture for 2015.

Photo Simon De Rudder

The local team led by Guy has put the ball in motion by repainting the simulator in its original Flying Tigers livery and conducting a complete technical assessment to be accurate and realistic. Manuals and information have been collected so far although at the time of writing, Guy is still on the lookout for original Link wiring diagrams in order to develop an interface with a DC-8 flight simulator software. Programming, research, planning and conversion is very complex and requires time, patience, financial support and know-how. A new visual system will be installed using a large wraparound digital screen. Due to the complexity of this phase of the project, there is no timeframe for completion, however it will remain a labour of love for Guy and the team.

Inside the Flying Tigers DC-8 Simulator

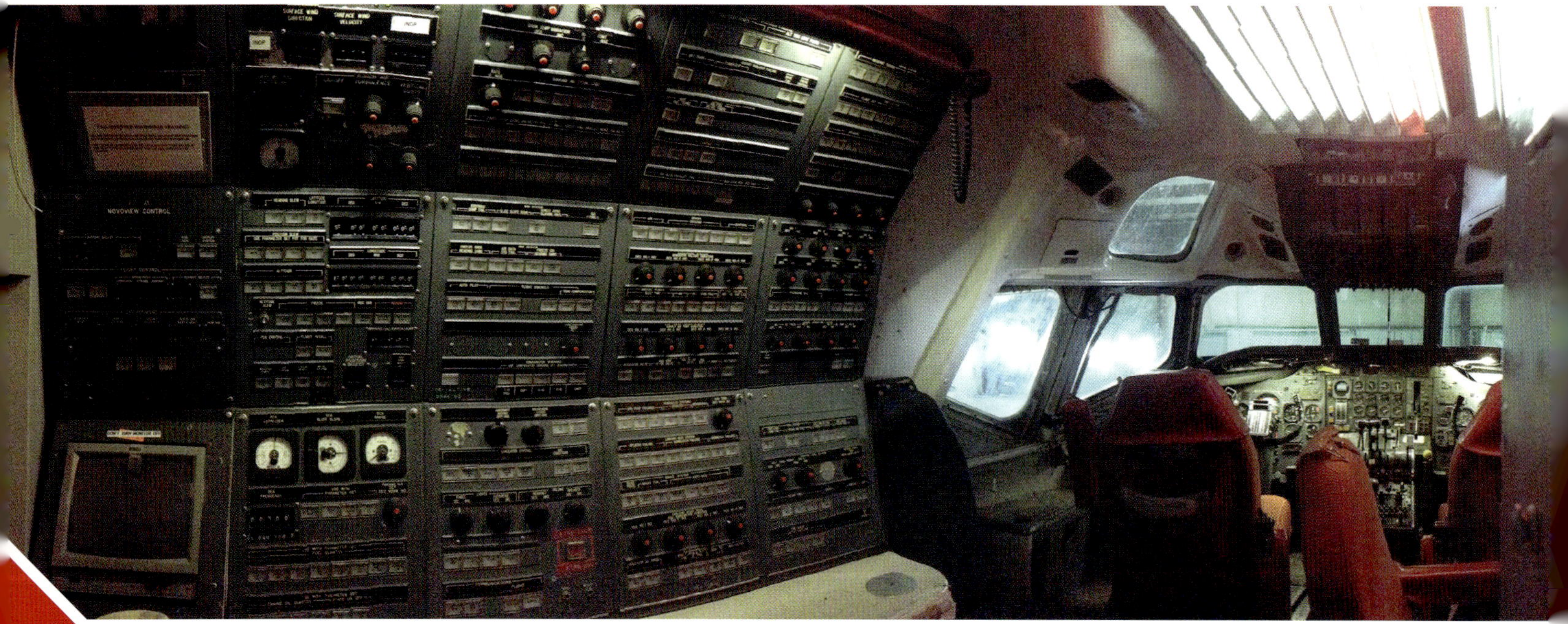

The instructor's console

Photos by Steve Cannaby

7 THREE YEARS OFF THIS EARTH:

Tales of flying the DC-8-63, Captain Mike Sweeley

Where to begin? I guess the best answer is to begin at the beginning. It's a bright and sunny day in mid-April 1965. There I am, a young cocky 22 year-old kid with a wet multi ticket in my back pocket. I am standing at the end of Sherman Way Blvd looking through the Burbank Airport gate at the tarmac opposite hangar #5. Across the top of that hangar is a sign which reads "The Flying Tiger Line".

Inside I can see a bustle of activity around the biggest airplane I have ever seen up close, a Lockheed Constellation L-1049H. Its four Wright 3350 turbo-compound engine cowlings are all laid out on the hangar floor as guys in blue shirts and coveralls buzz around the engines like bees. I am wide-eyed and awestruck. Perhaps after today I'll be allowed to lay my hands on that hallowed collection of rivets known as the "Super Connie".

I was just a kid who in 1965 had listened to President Kennedy tell every American and the entire world that we were going to the moon and that all Americans were special people who could achieve whatever their imagination could conjure. And my dream was to fly airplanes!

I walked the quarter-mile back down the road to the company headquarters, impressive to me but by today's standards it would have been nothing of interest, but as I was soon to find out, it would become my company headquarters.

Today was Monday. I was here at the behest of a gruff white-haired aviation legend who I had impressed sufficiently on the previous Friday to warrant being given a shot at securing a seat in Flying Tigers' first class of pilots that year. The class of April 1965.

I can remember, to this day, sitting that Friday in front of grey-haired Johnny Holmes. On his desk in front of him was a sign which declared his awesome power and position: Chief Pilot. The arrogant 22 year-old whippersnapper dressed in his only suit sat quivering.

Will I be able to justify and explain every one of my logbook entries, will I be able to recite from rote each and every emergency procedure of every airplane listed therein? His first question took me by surprise and most certainly broke the ice. "Tell me, Mike. Why do you want to fly?"

That was it. He had me. This gruff and likable guy had become a god to me. By today's standards the interview was short and to the point, of pleasant discussion about airplanes with sly points thrown in requiring me to demonstrate my aviation expertise. I did not realize it that day but during all this light discussion I was being evaluated by one of the best. It was he and he alone who would determine my fate that day. No HR interviews, no interview boards, no simulator evaluations, just thumbs up or down from this awesome man.

One hour later Holmes paused and looked out the window over the hangar floor. He thought for a moment while I held my breath, then turned to look at me and said, "Go downstairs and tell the lady at the reception desk that I want you to report for class Monday morning, and if she gives you any shit tell her to call me!" That was it!

Later that day, sitting around the boardroom table in the old Sherman Way offices with thirty other hopefuls, all silent, all deep in our thoughts. I can remember and see all the faces in my mind today although some of the names slip my memory... Fred Lynch, George Gewehr, Lee Bray, Bill Popp, Ted Freedell, Dick Hill, Jim Theobald, Dwight Small, Dennis King,

Bob Baird and Brian Ferris. All these great men would become my friends and fellow Tiger pilots.

We were told by some geek that we were going to be given, for the first time in company history, the Stanine Test, but not to worry, ours would be the yardstick by which later classes would be evaluated. Off we went, one whole day of silly questions from some guy who had no idea how to fly an airplane. None of us were worried.

Tuesday arrived and I waited eagerly by the telephone, staring at it, demanding it ring. At 11am it complied. The voice on the other end told me to report to the classroom on the second floor of Hangar 5 the following day at 8am to begin class on the "Super Connie". I had made it. My dream had come true.

Wednesday dawned dreary, but I did not care – I was on cloud nine. There we all were, about twenty of us, our ranks thinned because the company had decided to enforce stringent Stanine guidelines after all, and that some had not met that hurtle. (So much for being a guideline!)

We sat with bated breath. What would this day hold for each of us? We soon found out: as our names were called we were told to either sit in the chairs on the right or the chairs on the left. Soon a crusty old guy appeared, who we would later learn was the legendary Chief Engineer Roy McClain. He stood before us and with a wave of his hand, sealed all of our fates for years to come. Those of us on the left row of seats, because they had completed their flight

engineers' written exam, would be flight engineers; those of us on the right row, because we had not taken the engineers written, me included, would be co-pilots. The die had been cast, our fate was sealed.

With that, Roy McLain turned to the business at hand. Flash: projected on the screen at the front of the classroom was a picture of a voluptuous naked lady. Boy, this pilot thing is not bad at all, I thought. Roy smiled and said, "Gentlemen, take a good look, because for the next three weeks this is what you are going to get intimately familiar with!" and up popped a schematic diagram of the Wright 3350 fuel control unit in all its glory and total mystery. And thus began my love affair with Tigers, a part of my heart and memory which only men of old age and wisdom can appreciate.

Before I move on to DC-8 tales, please allow me one story, one which I will never forget as long as I live: my very first flight on the line. I had finished my training and just the previous day taken a check ride as co-pilot for the fabled check captain of Israeli Air force fame, Wayne Peak. That afternoon I was told my first flight would the following night from FTL's LAX facility to SFO.

The captain was Jim Cullen. Wait, I thought. I don't even have a uniform! Nevertheless, there I was, spit and polish the following night, dressed in my suave 1960s leisure suit awaiting the arrival of Captain Cullen who would guide me through the confusing maze of preflight paperwork and flight planning.

But it was not to be so. Forty minutes before the flight was to leave, the operations agent called me over to the crew room window. All eyes in that room that night were on the newbie – I was sweating! Captain Cullen would be late and he requested that I file the flight plan and finish the paperwork and he would meet me at the airplane.

Oh my god. I could not find the seat lever or the gear handle. How could I complete the paperwork?

But complete it I did. Jim never said a thing so I guess I got something right that night. Flight engineer Ed Herbert was already in his seat doing his thing on the engineer's panel so

I introduced myself. Before Ed could say hello back, in came Jim. He hauled the left seat back, climbed in, introduced himself with a sly grin and asked Ed and I if we were ready to go. Ed simply nodding in agreement, and I said in dry voice, "Yes sir!"

After getting all the ground clearances, Captain Cullen commanded, "Start number 3!" I sat there dumbfounded. A tap on my shoulder from Ed brought me back to reality. "Would you mind looking out the window, boy, and telling me when we have six blades," he asked.

Opening the side window I hung my head out and waited. The 3350 propeller began to turn and as I counted six blades, Ed yelled "Contact!", blue flame erupted from the exhaust stacks, and with a mighty roar, the eighteen-cylinder Wright leapt into life.

Since the Tiger LAX facility was at the end of runway 25 Right, we had a very short taxi. "Tiger 916, taxi into position, you are cleared for takeoff," the tower radioed. Oh my god, I thought, where is the gear handle, where is the check list, what next? I was terrified I would screw up. Captain Cullen lined up on the runway, set the brakes, slid his seat back, lit a cigar then turned to me and said those words every copilot wants to hear: "It's your leg!"

I was petrified. But off we went to SFO: one confident Captain and one lost copilot. Approaching our descent point into SFO, Jim leaned over to me and whispered in my ear something I will never forgot: "Boy," he said, "I want you to remember one thing. You are the pilot and this guy behind you is a flight engineer. You fly the airplane and he does what you tell him to do. So I want to hear you bark those orders on final approach to him just so he knows who runs the show around here. Now let's hear it: RICH and 2400!" And so began the first day of rest of my twenty-five year career with Flying Tigers.

Years passed and so did airplanes. Super Connie, Canadair CL-44, Boeing 707, then finally the queen of the fleet, the last aircraft actually built by Douglas Aircraft before it was acquired by McDonnell Aircraft. It was the last of a proud line which had started with the DC-2 and of course the infamous DC-3, many of which are still flying up here in my state of Alaska today. During the war, the DC-4 workhorse came along, followed afterward, mostly in commercial service, by the DC-6 and DC-7. The line culminated, in my humble opinion, with one of the best aircraft ever designed: the DC-8.

Along with FTL's decision to acquire the stretched DC-8-63 came the need to upgrade many crews to the airplane. My chance was now; as I remember, I won the last captain's seat on that bid. An airline pilots dream, captain of my own ship! And thus in 1980 I was flying the DC-8 as a captain and hence a tale of two very interesting trips!

In the 1982 to 1985 era, Tigers had ventured into the cargo charter business big time and the company proposed that due to contract requirements they wanted to establish a separate pilot domicile, a sort of domicile within a domicile whose purpose was to fly the contract requirements and use FAR rules only as guidelines. ALPA agreed and thus came into being "Wallace's Cowboys".

Ned Wallace, the VP of charter operations, now had twenty crews which in essence belonged strictly to him. I think he knew exactly the type of crews he would get, the kind he needed for such an undertaking. Every one of those twenty crews were well suited for the job, all type-A personalities: bold, self-reliant and adventurers at heart. We all took to the job like ducks to water. Thus begins my soliloquy of two rather distinctive trips.

Tigers had contracted with Panalpina Cargo for five round-trips to Lagos in Nigeria; two crews had been assigned the duty. Based in Palma de Majorca off the coast of Spain, one crew would fly each day up to Europe to pick up a load and return, while the other crew would fly from Palma de Majorca to Lagos.

My crew and I had drawn the southbound duty; my copilot was Jim Camp, my engineer Jean-Claude Demirdjian. We left the first night thinking that this would be a piece of cake, and would be back in time to enjoy breakfast on the hotel veranda overlooking the blue Mediterranean Sea by morning. We had overlooked one thing in the flight plan: we had no overfly permit number for the People's Republic of Benin (present day Republic of Benin). A problem to be sure, but not unsolvable if you have the right crew!

Benin was a former French colony and thus two truisms applied: they did not like Americans, and they spoke French. Flying at 37,000 feet, we crossed into Benin airspace and proceeded to give their air traffic control in the capital city of Cotonou a call with a position report; now the fun began. Cotonou promptly replied asking for our "permit number"; which we did not have. At which point, in the dark of the night, they demanded that we land immediately. I was on the radio trying to soft-peddle the problem while Jim Camp scrambled to find Cotonou International Airport approach plates in the ship's library.

At this point it was Jean Claude to the rescue – as many of you may remember, Jean-Claude is of Armenian ancestry and immigrated to France and finally to America where he became an air force pilot. Of course Jean Claude speaks three languages – Armenian, French and English, and voila a solution presented itself. With harsher and harsher demands coming from Cotonou to our headsets, Jean-Claude picked up the microphone and, as Jim and I watched in awe, began conversing with the controller in French. For five minutes this went on, with Jim and I completely oblivious to what was being said. Jean-Claude eventually hung up the microphone, lookied at me he said, "Captain, we are clear to proceed!"

DEMIRDJIAN, Jean-Claude

What had just happened? Jim and I were dumbfounded. What had Jean-Claude said to change this Cassandra into a personable person of bonhomie nature? With a sparkle in his eye, Jean-Claude explained he had told the controller that although this was a US-registered aircraft, the crew was totally French, as witnessed by his total command of the French language, and that we were on a mission of mercy, flying 90,000 lbs of Bordeaux wine to French refugees awaiting evacuation from the Nigeria civil war. When asked by Jean-Claude what they would have done if we had not complied with their previous demands, the controller politely said, "Nothing, we have nothing which could go high enough to shoot you down." With a tip of his fedora and a push of the microphone button, Jean-Claude bade Cotonou farewell: "Bonne chance mes amis!" Good luck my friends. Thus the Tiger sprit of 'can do" manifested itself again in wonderful crews aboard a great airplane.

My second treatise with regard to the DC-8 begins in Italy. My crew and I had flown into Pisa as passengers into position for a trip. Arriving at the airport the evening of the following day, we met our loadmaster Ted Schmitt. Ted briefed me on the mission and the load: 98,000 lbs of Colt M16 rifles bound for Kinshasa, Zaire. This was government-issue "foreign aid" to Zaire who at that moment were fighting Cuban-backed communist Angola. I mused to Ted, why were we picking these guns up in Italy?

His explanation made all things perfectly clear. President Carter had recently declared that America would no long involve itself in foreign adventures, which had immediately forced the Colt arms factory to initiate a move to Pisa, Italy. Well, don't blame me; I have a bridge to sell you!

The takeoff that evening in cool fifty degree temperatures was uneventful and typically laid-back Italian. "Tiger 457, turn left, climb and call Rome Control". Settling down at cruise altitude, we awaited dawn over the Mediterranean Sea and our scheduled fuel stop at Tripoli, Libya, the old Wheeler Air Force base, at around 11:30am local time. Piece of cake? Wrong!

FTL 747 Captain Jean-Claude Démirdjian in the 80's

There it was on final approach shimmering in the sun: Tripoli's two 12,000 foot runways. Touchdown was uneventful and we taxied to the deserted ramp and shut the engines down as an Arab man ambled out to plug in the GPU. Ted opened the door and immediately everyone in the cockpit looked at one another. Two big problems presented themselves immediately: one, Libya was on Angola's side in this war; and two, no one had anticipated at flight planning back at LAX that the ramp temperatures would be in excess of 125F.

The first order of business was to keep the air-conditioning packs running and the door closed so that no Libyan ground personal could see enough inside the aircraft to know what we were really carrying.

Ted slipped out to pay the fuel vender in cash. We had correctly assumed, as was later confirmed, that if they had known what was on board the aircraft we would have spent a long time in a Libyan jail, with zero help from the US government (a DC-8? we know nothing of a stinking DC-8!).

And then it was decision time. My crew and I huddled. Do we stay here until nightfall and lower temperatures and take the chance of getting caught? Or do we fly no matter what the takeoff charts say? We all agreed. Tiger can-do spirit took over.

Laying the long fold-out takeoff performance chart on the floor of the cockpit, we extrapolated a line far off the printed chart where takeoff run and second segment climb intersected with the 125F temperature line. With bubble gum and black marker we determined that with 12,000 feet of runway and 400 miles of low-rise Saharan desert sand dunes ahead of us, we could climb at just 100 feet per minute, just enough to clear the highest dune in our path.

Off we went as fast as possible, starting engines and getting taxi instructions. I lined up on the centerline; ahead of me lay 12,000 feet of concrete shimmering in noonday heat. The flight engineer informed me that most likely we would be temperature limited on takeoff but he would do his best to give us all he could muster from the engines.

With that in mind I called "max power!", released the brakes, and the big -63 began to roll slowly down the runway, gradually accelerating. It seemed an eternity before the copilot yelled "V1!", then "Rotate!" As I pulled back on the yoke, I saw out of the corner of my eye the 11,000 foot marker flash past. Airborne with just 100 feet of paved surface to spare, clawing at the sky, sand dunes whizzing by our windows, the vertical speed barely showed 100 feet per minute.

The sound of those Pratt and Whitneys purring flawlessly was music to our ears. About ten miles out, we had enough speed and I called, "Flaps up." We were home free, climbing into the bright Arabian sky; Douglas Aircraft Company had once again never let us down and the Tiger spirit lived on.

Well that is it; tales of ghostly DC-8s and days gone by. Soon, all of those who belonged to Wallace's Cowboys will have flown west, but I can assure you that myself and all those I speak for will never forget the "Tiger Can-Do", the Wallace's Cowboys and the marvelous company who gave us the Douglas DC-8 model 63.

Blue Skies and tailwinds to all!
Captain Mike Sweeley, FTL 19199
April 1965 to July 2003

THE NASA DC-8

In 2015, the last DC-8 flying under US-registration is NASA's N817NA, a DC-8-72 originally delivered to Alitalia on May 14, 1969 as I-DIWK, Ship 458 off the line at Long Beach. The aircraft went to Braniff on January 5, 1982, was bought by NASA via Cammacorp in January 1986 to replace a Convair 990 and was converted to a -72 by Delta.

Several years were spent on modifications to turn Ship 458 into a flying laboratory, including the ability to carry up to 30,000 lbs (13,608 kgs) of scientific instruments and equipment, including Inmarsat satellite communications capability, two Iridium communications systems (one for flight crew communications and one for science team communications), and a multichannel system for upload of meteorological data and data telemetry.

Initially based at Moffett Field, between Mountain View and Sunnyvale, near San Jose in northern California, today N817NA flies out of Palmdale outside Los Angeles participating in experiments in support of projects serving the global scientific community, in fields as diverse and wide-ranging as (deep breath…) archaeology, ecology, geography, hydrology, meteorology, oceanography, volcanology, atmospheric chemistry, cryospheric science, soil science, and biology. More specifically, and closer to home for NASA, the ship is used for collecting data related to America's space missions, mostly in the field of satellite sensor verifica-

tion and space vehicle launch or re-entry telemetry data (retrieval and optical tracking).

Starting in 1991, NASA made a conscious move towards a comprehensive program to study the Earth as an environmental system; in an excellent example of how space missions and Earth science dovetail, the DC-8 conducted the Active Sensing Of CO2 Emissions Over Nights, Days and Seasons II campaign during the summer of 2011, supporting tests with four laser instruments used to gather remote measurements of atmospheric carbon dioxide. Flights were flown over different land features from desert to snow, testing surface reflectance effects on instrument performance. Space-borne lasers would find the same type of surfaces when used to study components of Earth's atmosphere from space. This research contributes to further development of laser-based Earth-observing satellite instruments designed to measure atmospheric carbon dioxide.

Because it is flown in the Earth's atmosphere, the N817NA offers a comparatively inexpensive way to test and verify prototype satellite instruments. Scientists use the DC-8 to develop ideas in instrument technology as well as to test new instruments and modify them if necessary based on flight results. Potential problems can be corrected before new instruments are launched into space. As a result, flight-proven hardware can lead to substantial savings in time and resources.

Once in orbit, satellite instruments send back billions of data bits daily. To help scientists calibrate the accuracy of data obtained, the DC-8 flies under a satellite's path, using instruments to compile the same information as that collected by the satellite. Through this process, algorithms used to interpret satellite data are evaluated and updated to reflect the results verified with DC-8 instrumentation.

A tracking antenna used in receiving launch vehicle telemetry data was installed in the nose of the DC-8 to support launches of the Missile Defense Agency's Space Tracking And Surveillance Demonstration satellites, and NASA's Glory Earth science satellite.

Over Weddell Sea *Photo: NASA / Michael Studinger*

The DC-8 has also successfully supported optical tracking missions of spacecraft re-entering the Earth's atmosphere. Two examples are the re-entry of the European Automated Transfer Vehicle Jules Verne in 2008, and the 2010 the re-entry of the Japan Aerospace Exploration Agency's Hayabusa spacecraft.

In 2009 the DC-8 began participation in Operation Ice Bridge, NASA's annual polar ice field campaign, with flights over Antarctica from a deployment base at Punta Arenas, Chile. The aircraft carries researchers and their instruments over western and northern Antarctica in the largest airborne survey ever flown of Earth's polar ice. During March and April 2010, the DC-8 was based in Greenland for Ice Bridge's Arctic ice study. Ice Bridge's airborne research continues the multi-year measurements started by NASA's Ice, Cloud And Land Elevation Satellite (ICE-Sat-I), which ceased operation in 2009, and will fill the gap alone until ICESat-II is launched in 2016.

The twelve-hour endurance and range of the DC-8-72 combined with the four-engine reliability makes N817NA able to wander far and wide from it's southern California base in search of new scientific missions for the benefit of us all. With plenty of life left in the airframe, North America's last DC-8 will be flying high for many years to come.

NASA DC-8 was originally delivered to Alitalia as I-DIWK in 1969

NASA DC-8-72H with its first registration N717NA

Turning finals for Palmdale regional airport

Photo Geoffrey Thomas